Vegetarian Feasts

Richard Cawley
Vegetarian Feasts
Memorable Meat-Free Menus

Photography by
Debbie Patterson

Crescent Books
New York · Avenel

For Joan Campbell

Unless stated otherwise, all menus and recipes serve 6 people.
Spoon measurements are level unless otherwise stated.

Editorial Direction: Lewis Esson Publishing
Art Direction: Mary Evans
Design: Alison Fenton
Food for Photography: Richard Cawley with Ian Hands; Jane
    Suthering
Editorial Assistant: Penny David
Production: Clare Coles

This 1995 edition is published by Crescent Books,
distributed by Random House Value Publishing, Inc.
40 Engelhard Avenue
Avenel, New Jersey 07001

Random House
New York ● Toronto ● London ● Sydney ● Auckland

Typeset by Servis Filmsetting Ltd, Manchester, U.K.
Printed and bound by Wing King Tong Co Ltd, Hong Kong

A CIP catalog record for this book is available from the
Library of Congress.

ISBN 0-517-14237-6

8 7 6 5 4 3 2 1

Contents

LIST OF MENUS

LIST OF RECIPES

To enable you to create menus of your own, the recipes in the book are set out below categorized by course and occasion. Obviously many dishes may appear in more than one category—and readers may also find their very own uses for dishes which do not appear in our listing.

Unless stated otherwise, each recipe has been devised to serve 6 as an appetizer, main course, or accompaniment in its menu. If the dish is to be used in a different role, quantities may have to be scaled up or down appropriately.

INTRODUCTION

Vegetarianism is undoubtedly growing in popularity. People are giving up meat —and even perhaps fish—for different reasons, including moral, ecological, and health issues. While this book certainly does not contain any recipes for meat or fish, it is not concerned with why anyone might choose a vegetarian diet. Indeed, although this book is filled with recipes acceptable to most vegetarians, it is intended not for vegetarians only, but for everyone who loves good food.

Until recently it was almost impossible for vegetarians to find anything acceptable and palatable to eat on most mainstream restaurant menus—except for the ubiquitous omelet and salad. Times are changing at long last, and many good restaurants now routinely offer a choice of vegetarian dishes. More often than not, however, I find restaurants catering specifically to vegetarians still produce heavy "brown" food with a surprising emphasis on fat-laden pastries and sugar-filled cakes and desserts. Perhaps as a result of this, vegetarianism is only just beginning to throw off its image of hippies, dry "nut roasts" and anonymous "savory bakes."

Fashion in food seems to change almost as quickly as it does in clothing. How many of us cook a favorite recipe time and time again and then find that a few months later it has been totally dropped from our repertoire? Nevertheless, vegetarian food generally seems to be stuck in the '60s and '70s, whereas nonvegetarian food has evolved into a much lighter, healthier, and more varied style of eating. In the same way, many vegetarian cookbooks are still written by authors whose prime interest is in the avoidance of meat and meat products, rather than the love of—and a wish to produce—good food.

Although I am not a vegetarian, I have never been a consumer of large amounts of meat—particularly red meat. In 1986 I wrote a book called *Not Quite Vegetarian*, which included reasonable quantities of poultry and fish. Such a strategy is now being universally advised by doctors and nutritionists as part of a healthier lifestyle. Adopting these recommendations, however, means not just eating less red meat, but also consuming less fat and sugar and much more fresh fruit and vegetables and fiber-rich foods like potatoes, pasta, bread, beans, and legumes.

What prompted me to write *Vegetarian Feasts* is that, when I give a dinner party these days, I often find that at least one of my guests will request not to be served any meat—and often not any fish either. To provide a separate menu for vegetarian guests not only makes additional work for the cook, but also makes the guest embarrassingly aware of being the cause of this extra trouble.

The simple answer is to cook such a delicious meatless meal for everyone that no one will mind—or even notice—that they are eating a "vegetarian" meal.

SOURCES OF INSPIRATION

When I decided to write this book I began to compile a list of possible recipe ideas that might be included, with dishes of every kind—simple and sophisticated, traditional and modern and inspired by cuisines from all around the world. Unfortunately, my list of ideas soon grew long enough to fill a book in itself, so I realized that some kind of editing was necessary. To this end I searched for a particular theme around which to plan the menus.

For the past few years I have been fortunate to spend three to four months of each year traveling, and I invariably choose to head south for guaranteed sunshine. Not only do I like the look and the feel of sunshine, but I like what it does to the people who live under it—and, perhaps more importantly, what it does to their food.

I love the flavors of the Mediterranean region—of France, Italy, Greece, and Turkey—and I have explored the scenery and food in many parts of these countries over the years. The last few long summers, however, I have spent in a magical French valley on the borders of Provence and the Languedoc. This region of goat cheese and honey, sunflower fields, vineyards, and hillsides covered with aromatic wild herbs and purple-cushioned rows of lavender enchanted me so greatly that I recently bought a house there.

It is in these happy surroundings that I enjoy shopping, cooking, and eating almost more than anywhere else in the world—except, that is, for Australia, where for the past six Christmases I have escaped the dreariness of gray northern winters for a month of Mediterranean-style summer "down under".

MY ANTIPODEAN MUSE

More than a few quizzical eyebrows have been raised when I extol the virtues of modern Australian cooking. However, such sceptics are people who have never visited that sunny continent. Sydney and the other cities are full of the most wonderful eating possibilities. Restaurants of every kind serve superb, well-cooked, and affordable food. Moreover, home cooks prepare delicious modern food which makes the most of the spectacular variety of top-quality Australian produce. Today's Australian cook also entertains with a style of informal sophistication that would bring sighs of admiration from hosts and hostesses everywhere. (Australians also make friends easily, so you won't have to wait long for invitations.)

This high standard of home cooking and entertaining owes much to the excellent quality of food journalism in Australia, in particular the food and entertaining pages of *Vogue Australia* publications and the extraordinary talent of their food editor of many years who is, in my opinion, perhaps the best food editor in the world.

Joan Campbell is a brilliant cook and journalist, with a unerring visionary eye for what will be the next trend in food. Joan's food pages—with their sparkling new ideas for things to cook that will both delight and impress your guests, be quick and easy to prepare, and, above all, look and taste superb—rekindle even the most jaded of appetites.

Luckily my antipodean muse of many years is now a firm friend, although when it comes to swapping recipes on the telephone I sometimes wish she were the food editor of a magazine somewhat closer to home.

THE COOK'S KITCHEN

Professional chefs are expected to spend many long hours in the kitchen. However, this should not necessarily be the case for home cooks. Cooking should be a pleasure, not a chore. The recipes in this book are therefore as quick and simple as I can make them.

Although it is perfectly possible to cook good food using only a few pans, a sharp knife, and a couple of spoons, certain kitchen "gadgets" are well worth the initial investment. I find two indispensable: the first is a good food processor, which saves hours and hours of boring work—chopping onions or grating bread crumbs by hand is not very creative and takes up time better spent on something more rewarding.

A good wok is invaluable for all kinds of cooking. Mine is my second invaluable kitchen "assistant." It is a superb lidded version, which is very heavy and—while having the traditional curved interior—is cleverly designed with a flat bottom on the outside so that it sits comfortably and safely on any heat source.

THE SHOPPING BASKET

Little irritates me more than reading in the publicity blurb for some fashionable restaurant that the secret of the chef in the spotlight is that he ''uses only the freshest of ingredients in his cooking.'' There is nothing special about that. My mother has done so for years, as does anyone who pretends to have the slightest interest in food. Some meats, many cheeses and, of course, wines certainly improve with aging, but fresh vegetables should be just that. There is nothing else to say on the subject.

You will, however, see that my Basics chapter and all the recipes are ''highly seasoned'' with as much information as I can give on any unusual or interesting ingredients.

TO THE TABLE

The great thing about almost all vegetarian meals is that you can drink whatever you want without having to worry too much about matching wine to food. Obviously, however, a subtle and delicate white wine might be overpowered by a dish that is either very robust or spicy, and some purists also insist that few wines taste good with either asparagus or artichokes.

So take this book into the kitchen and allow it to help you think positively about vegetarian food. Its contents are not just meatless meals but mouthwatering menus made up of exciting ingredients filled with glorious flavors to bring their sunshine to your table even on the grayest of winter days. Happy cooking!

BREADS AND BASICS

As a food writer, I am constantly trying out and testing new recipes for breads and pastries, dressings, and basic sauces. In the end, however, when I want a quick loaf, foolproof pastry, or a perfect mayonnaise I can make in seconds, I always return time and time again to a handful of basic recipes.

This chapter contains these favorites—tried-and-true old friends that never fail and are versatile enough to be adapted into more elaborate recipes without fear.

Also included in this section are three quick-and-easy pâtés, which are great standbys to have in the refrigerator for all sorts of occasions, and three dips that can be made in minutes and may also be used as sauces or dressings.

HOMEMADE BREAD

My method for making bread is as simple and quick as I can make it. Rather than fiddling with putting dough in a conventional bread pan, I bake it on a baking sheet to produce rustic-looking country-style loaves.

I also use quick-rising active dry yeast and add it directly to the dry ingredients. This eliminates the time it takes to reconstitute conventional active dry yeast in water. If you are unfamiliar with quick-rising active dry yeast, the important thing to remember is to use very warm liquid—120° to 130°. If the liquid is not this warm the yeast will not work. Take care, however, because if the liquid is too hot, it will "kill" the yeast.

The brand of yeast I use requires only one rising. Read the directions on your yeast packaging carefully. If the manufacturers suggest two risings, take their advice and adjust this recipe.

Makes 1 large loaf

6 **cups WHITE BREAD FLOUR (FOR A WHITE LOAF) OR 3 cups WHITE BREAD FLOUR WITH 3 cups OF WHOLE-WHEAT FLOUR (FOR A BROWN LOAF)**
1 **ENVELOPE (1 tbl.) QUICK-RISING ACTIVE DRY YEAST**
1½ **tsp. SALT**
1 **tbl. BUTTER OR SHORTENING**
2 **cups VERY WARM WATER (120° to 130°)**

Place the flour or flours in a large bowl with the yeast and salt. Cut in the butter or shortening as you would to make pie-crust dough, until the mixture resembles fine bread crumbs.

Stir in the warm water and bring the dough together to form a ball.

Place the dough on a floured counter and, holding the ball of dough at one side with one hand, stretch it away from you with the heel of your other hand, using a bashing and pushing movement. Continue to knead the dough this way for at least 10 minutes. Fold the dough in half, give the folded pile a quarter turn on the counter, and repeat the process.

Form the kneaded dough into a ball and place this on a floured board. Sprinkle the top with flour and cover it with floured plastic wrap or a floured lightweight cloth. Let it rise in a warm place (not too warm—just an average kitchen temperature will do!), until double in size; it is best to leave the dough to rise slowly rather than to force it on top of a hot stove, for instance. Make sure the dough is not in a draft. I find it also usually takes longer for the dough to rise than it indicates on the yeast package, and the actual time will depend on temperature, humidity, and so on: allow 2 to 3 hours.

Toward the end of this time, preheat the oven to 450°. Place a metal baking sheet on a middle shelf and a small heatproof bowl of boiling water on the bottom of the oven to provide humidity.

When the oven is really hot and the dough is fully risen, sprinkle the dough with a little more flour and quickly make 2 slashes across the top to form a cross which will help release any uneven tensions in the dough as it bakes, producing a nice, evenly shaped loaf. It also gives the bread a homemade look.

With a quick flicking motion, put the loaf onto the hot baking sheet in the oven. Close the door, and bake for 15 minutes. Turn down the oven temperature to 375° and let bake for 30 minutes. When properly baked, the loaf will have a brown crust and should sound "hollow" when tapped on the bottom.

"FASHIONABLE" LITTLE BREAD ROLLS

Makes 48

It is a pleasant fashion in popular restaurants these days to serve a variety of very small bread rolls with different flavors. These are very easy to make yourself from the basic bread dough on page 15.

Begin by dividing the basic quantity of dough in half and trying two of the flavorings suggested in the next column. Later you can go on to create your own flavors—the variations are endless.

Mix in the flavoring ingredients after the dough has been kneaded for 10 minutes. When you begin to mix in the flavorings, especially the oily ones such as olives and sun-dried tomatoes, it will seem difficult at first—if not impossible. If you persevere, however, after a couple of minutes of kneading the dough will "accommodate" the chosen flavoring.

Once you have kneaded in the extra flavoring ingredients to each half of the basic dough, divide each into 24 equal portions. Roll these into balls. Dip the tops in water and then in a topping, if you are using one.

Arrange the rolls on greased baking sheets (when making many rolls it is not possible to flick them onto a hot baking sheet as I suggest with the large loaf), leaving enough room between each roll for the dough to rise. Cover with floured plastic wrap or a cloth and let them rise until they have doubled in size.

Bake the rolls in an oven preheated to 425° for 10 to 15 minutes, until risen and golden.

For the photograph we made four different kinds of rolls. Some we simply left plain and others we dipped briefly in cold water and then in sesame seeds or oatmeal, before leaving them to rise.

Flavorings and toppings:
1. To half the quantity of basic dough made with all white bread flour, mix in about ½ cup chopped walnuts.

   Top half of these with oatmeal.
2. To half the quantity of basic dough made with all white bread flour, mix in ⅓ cup drained and chopped sun-dried tomatoes in oil, 2 tsp. concentrated tomato paste, and ½ tsp. dried oregano.
3. To half the quantity of basic dough made with equal parts white bread and whole-wheat flours, mix in 1 crushed garlic clove and 2 tbl. of finely chopped parsley.
4. To half the quantity of basic dough made with equal parts white bread and whole-wheat flours, mix in ½ cup pitted and finely chopped olives.

   Top half of these with sesame seeds.

WALNUT SODA BREAD

This tasty variation on Irish soda bread uses milk and yogurt instead of the traditional buttermilk. It also includes added walnuts for extra crunch and flavor. The best thing about this bread, however, is that it takes only minutes to prepare.

Makes 1 large loaf
3 cups WHOLE-WHEAT FLOUR
3 cups WHITE BREAD FLOUR
½ tsp. SALT
1 tbl. BAKING SODA
2 tbl. CREAM OF TARTAR
2 tsp. SUGAR
1 cup WALNUTS, COARSELY CHOPPED
1 cup LOW-FAT PLAIN YOGURT
1½ cups MILK
VEGETABLE OIL FOR GREASING

Preheat the oven to 425°. Grease a baking sheet with oil.

In a large bowl, combine the dry ingredients. In another bowl, beat together the yogurt and milk until combined. Stir this mixture into the dry ingredients and mix together with a fork.

Put the dough (which will be fairly soft and moist) onto a floured counter. Using well-floured hands, bring it together into a ball.

Place this on the prepared baking sheet and pat it out to a circle about 1¼ inches thick. Cut the circle into quarters and push these apart so there is a thin gap (the width of a pencil) between each. Dust the top with flour. Bake immediately for 30 minutes until each quarter sounds hollow when tapped on the bottom.

This bread is best eaten on the same day it is baked.

CORN BREAD

There are lots of recipes for different versions of corn bread. This is my version, which probably isn't authentic but is quite delicious and takes only a few minutes to make.

Look in health-food stores and specialty delicatessens for stoneground cornmeal, which is slightly coarser than the commercial, readily available yellow variety.

You can also use "easy-cook" polenta, which is readily available from Italian food stores and delicatessens. It is pretty much the same thing.

Makes 1 loaf
4 tbl. BUTTER, MELTED
1 cup LOW-FAT PLAIN YOGURT
½ cup MILK
2 EGGS, BEATEN
1 cup CORNMEAL (SEE INTRODUCTION)
½ cup ALL-PURPOSE FLOUR
1 tsp. SALT
2 tbl. SUGAR
1 tbl. BAKING POWDER
GOOD PINCH (⅛ tsp.) OF BAKING SODA

Banana Bread

Preheat the oven to 400°. Grease an 8-×4-×2½-inch bread pan with a little of the butter.

In one large bowl, mix together all the liquid ingredients. In another bowl, mix together all the dry ingredients.

Quickly, and using as few strokes of a spoon as possible, fold the wet ingredients into the dry ingredients.

Pour this batter into the prepared pan. Bake for 35 minutes, or until a toothpick pushed into the middle of the loaf comes out clean.

Let cool, then slice.

BANANA BREAD

Makes 1 loaf

½ cup BUTTER, PLUS MORE FOR GREASING

3 cups SELF-RISING FLOUR

½ tsp. SALT

1 tsp. CINNAMON

¾ cup PACKED LIGHT BROWN SUGAR

3 EGGS, BEATEN

3 LARGE BANANAS, 1 lb., PEELED AND MASHED OR PURÉED IN A BLENDER OR FOOD PROCESSOR (ABOUT 3 cups)

Preheat the oven to 375°. Grease an 8-×4-×2½-inch bread pan with butter and line the bottom with waxed paper.

Put the flour, salt, and cinnamon in a large bowl. Mix together.

Put the sugar in another large bowl. Melt the butter, not letting it get too hot. Pour it over the sugar and mix together.

Gradually beat in the eggs. Add the flour mixture, followed by the bananas and mix together.

Pour this batter into the prepared pan. Bake for 50 to 60 minutes, or until a toothpick inserted into the middle of the loaf comes out clean.

Leave the loaf in the pan for 10 minutes, then turn it out, peel off the paper, and let cool completely.

CHRISTINE'S SCONES

I thought my scones were pretty good, but my "big" sister (who always knows better) took me in hand and taught me how to make them the way she was taught.

The scones that follow are, I think—thanks to Christine—not far from perfection! They are best made fresh when you need them (which is not a problem because they take only a couple of minutes to make), but they do, however, freeze very well.

The first secret to making superior scones is not to have the mixture too dry, the second secret is to make them quickly and handle them as little as possible, and the third secret is not to overbake them.

Makes 8

4 tbl. BUTTER, CUT INTO SMALL PIECES, PLUS MORE FOR GREASING

2 cups SELF-RISING FLOUR

GOOD PINCH OF BAKING POWDER

PINCH OF SALT (MY ADDITION, THOUGH NOT STRICTLY TRADITIONAL)

1 tbl. SUGAR

⅔ cup MILK

Preheat the oven to 450°. Lightly grease a baking sheet with some butter.

Sift the flour into a bowl. Add the baking powder, salt, and sugar. Cut in the butter, as if making piecrust dough, until the mixture resembles fine bread crumbs.

Using a fork, quickly mix in the milk to make a soft dough. (This can also all be done in seconds in a food processor.)

Put the dough onto a lightly floured counter and quickly draw it together into a ball. Flour your hands well because the dough will be very soft and quickly pat the dough out to about ½ inch thick.

Using a 2½-inch round cookie cutter, cut out 6 circles. Quickly draw together the trimmings, pat the dough out again, and cut out 2 more circles.

Arrange the scones on the prepared baking sheet. Bake for 8 to 10 minutes, until risen and golden. Serve immediately.

PIECRUST DOUGH

There are so many different kinds of pastry doughs, but time and time again I return to this recipe which works perfectly for most sweet and savory dishes. It is quick to make, easy to roll out, and behaves very well when baked, being light and crisp but not too fragile.

I have given the traditional method for making it by hand here, but I always make my dough in a food processor because it takes only seconds.

Makes about 14 ounces
2 cups ALL-PURPOSE FLOUR
¾ tsp. SALT
½ cup CHILLED BUTTER, CUT INTO SMALL
    PIECES
1 EGG YOLK, LIGHTLY BEATEN

Put the flour and salt in a mixing bowl. Cut in the butter until the mixture resembles fine bread crumbs.

Stir in the egg yolk and 3 tbl. of cold water. Working quickly, bring the mixture together until it forms a smooth dough.

Wrap in plastic wrap and chill for at least 30 minutes before use.

LIGHT VEGETABLE STOCK

Stock may be made from any kind of vegetables, and it is a good idea to make some when you have a surplus from your garden or the market.

There are, however, many good vegetable stock cubes available, which I sometimes use if I am in a hurry.

The quantities and ingredients given here are just a guide which you can adapt to whatever ingredients you have on hand. The onion skins will give your finished stock a lovely golden glow.

Makes about 2 quarts
1½ cups SLICED MUSHROOMS
1 lb. ONIONS, QUARTERED,
    BUT SKINS LEFT ON (SEE INTRODUCTION)
1½ cups COARSELY CHOPPED CARROTS
1½ cups COARSELY CHOPPED RUTABAGA,
    PARSNIP, OR TURNIP
3 GARLIC CLOVES
STRIP OF THINLY PARED PEEL FROM AN
    UNWAXED LEMON, ABOUT 2 INCHES LONG
LARGE BUNCH OF PARSLEY (COMPLETE WITH
    STEMS)
SMALL BUNCH OF OTHER HERBS AS AVAILABLE
1 BAY LEAF
2 tsp. SALT
1 tsp. SUGAR
PEPPER
GOOD DASH OF SOY SAUCE

Put all the ingredients in a large saucepan with 2½ quarts of water.

Bring to a boil, then simmer gently for 1½ hours.

Strain and discard the solids.

VINAIGRETTE

This is a basic recipe which can be varied according to taste or to suit the ingredients of the salad it is to dress.

Try different oils, such as walnut or hazelnut, or a mixture. Experiment with flavored vinegars or substitute lemon or lime juice. "Spike" your dressing with a little horseradish, crushed garlic, or chili instead of mustard, or add small quantities of chopped herbs.

Makes about 4 tbl.
1 tbl. WHITE-WINE VINEGAR
¼ tsp. SALT
GOOD TWIST OF FRESHLY GROUND
    BLACK PEPPER
½ tsp. SUGAR
¼ tsp. DRY MUSTARD
3 tbl. EXTRA-VIRGIN OLIVE OIL

Place the vinegar, salt, pepper, sugar, and mustard in a screw-top jar. Close the jar and shake until the sugar dissolves.

Add the oil and shake again until amalgamated. If possible, leave for 30 minutes to 1 hour before using to let the flavors develop.

Shake well again before using.

MAYONNAISE

All the worries of making homemade mayonnaise are taken away by using a food processor or blender. It never fails and takes no more time to make from scratch than it does to open a jar.

The flavor depends on the oil you use. A strong, fruity extra-virgin olive oil will naturally produce a strong, fruity flavored mayonnaise, which is especially good if converted into aïoli *with the addition of crushed garlic. If you want a milder flavor, however, use a milder-flavored oil or half olive oil and half flavorless vegetable oil.*

Makes about 1 cup
1 EGG (AT ROOM TEMPERATURE)
1 tsp. SALT
½ tsp. DRY MUSTARD
¾ cup OLIVE OIL (SEE INTRODUCTION)
PEPPER (WHITE IS PREFERABLE TO
    BLACK, WHICH PRODUCES LITTLE
    DARK SPECKS)
GOOD SQUEEZE OF LEMON JUICE

Put the egg, salt, and mustard in the bowl of a food processor or blender. Process until smooth.

With the motor still running, add the oil in a thin, steady trickle. You can pour a little faster as the mayonnaise starts to thicken.

Add pepper and lemon juice to taste. If the mayonnaise is too thick, add 1 to 2 tbl. of boiling water and blend briefly.

Mayonnaise in the gravy boat and Vinaigrette in the glass pitcher, together with an assortment of flavored oils and vinegars.

HOLLANDAISE SAUCE

One of the richest and most luxurious of all the classic French sauces, hollandaise is best reserved for special occasions—perhaps as a reward after a week of particularly healthy low-fat eating! It transforms any plainly cooked vegetable into a treat, and is really sublime with asparagus.

It is a notoriously tricky sauce to make. With the help of a blender or food processor, however, this "cheat's" version is child's play.

Makes about ⅔ cup
2 EGG YOLKS
1 tbl. LEMON JUICE
6 tbl. UNSALTED BUTTER
SALT AND PEPPER

Put the egg yolks, lemon juice, and 1 tsp. of water in the bowl of a food processor or blender. Whizz until well blended and frothy.

Meanwhile, melt the butter in a small saucepan until bubbling—but do not let it brown.

With the motor of the processor or blender still running, add the melted butter in a slow, steady stream. Continue to process for a few seconds longer. Season to taste.

Transfer the mixture to a double boiler or a heatproof bowl set over a pan of slowly simmering water. Stir constantly until thickened.

If you do not want to use the sauce immediately, keep it warm for up to 15 minutes simply by removing the pan from the stove and leaving the bowl sitting over the warm water. However, keep stirring occasionally for another minute or so, because it will continue to cook for a little while after you remove it from the heat.

CUMBERLAND SAUCE

This simple old-fashioned fruity sauce is traditionally associated with meat and meat pies, but is also perfect with all kinds of meatless dishes such as the Chestnut, Apple, and Onion Pie in the Christmas menu starting on page 26.

The sauce can be served hot or cold, but I prefer it cold.

Makes about 1 ¼ cups
1 UNWAXED LEMON
1 UNWAXED ORANGE
¼ tsp. DRY MUSTARD
6 DROPS OF HOT-PEPPER SAUCE OR A GOOD PINCH OF CAYENNE PEPPER
PINCH OF SALT
7 tbl. PORT WINE
⅓ cup RED CURRANT JELLY

Thinly pare the peel from half the lemon and half the orange. Cut these peels into the thinnest possible "needles." Blanch them in a small pan of boiling water for 5 minutes. Drain them, refresh in cold water, and drain again.

Squeeze the juice from the lemon and orange into a small pan. Stir in the mustard, hot-pepper sauce or cayenne, and salt and stir until dissolved. Add the port and the red currant jelly. Bring to a boil, then simmer for 5 minutes, or until the jelly completely dissolves.

Strain the sauce through a nonmetallic strainer into a pitcher or serving dish. Stir in the "needles" of blanched citrus peel. Reheat if serving hot, or let cool and chill if serving cold.

Cumberland Sauce

Put the shallots, wine, and vinegar in a small pan over low heat. Simmer until reduced to about 2 tbl. (This takes about 5 minutes, and must be done slowly to cook the shallot and let it give off its flavor.)

Over low to medium heat, whisk in the chilled butter, 2 pieces at a time (as soon each pair has melted, add 2 more). It should take 3 to 4 minutes to incorporate all the butter. If the sauce begins to bubble, remove the pan from the heat for a moment because the butter will become oily if it gets too hot. The finished sauce should be pale, creamy, and emulsified. Season to taste with salt and pepper.

The sauce should be served warm, and can be kept warm over a pan of simmering water for about 15 minutes.

BEURRE BLANC

Some cooks strain the shallots once they have given off their flavor, but I prefer to leave them in the finished sauce.

This sauce is perfect with all vegetables and many savory dishes.

Makes about 1 ¼ cups
2 SHALLOTS, FINELY CHOPPED
3 tbl. WHITE WINE
3 tbl. WHITE-WINE VINEGAR
1 cup CHILLED UNSALTED BUTTER, CUT INTO 1-inch CUBES
SALT AND PEPPER

HUMMUS

This popular Middle Eastern dip, made from garbanzo beans and tahini is available in delicatessens and supermarkets. With the aid of a blender or food processor, however, it takes seconds to make at home and is, of course, much less expensive.

Tahini is a paste made from sesame seeds. When you make tahini at home, don't overprocess it because the finished purée should have some texture.

Makes about 1 ¼ cups
2⅓ cups CANNED GARBANZO BEANS, DRAINED AND RINSED
1 GARLIC CLOVE, CRUSHED
4 tbl. TAHINI (SEE INTRODUCTION)
JUICE OF ½ LEMON
SALT
To garnish
1 tbl. OLIVE OIL
GOOD PINCH OF PAPRIKA
1 tsp. FINELY CHOPPED PARSLEY

Put the garbanzo beans, garlic, tahini, and lemon juice in the bowl of a food processor or blender. Process until smooth. Season to taste with salt.

Spoon the hummus into a serving dish. Smooth the surface with the back of a spoon. Drizzle with olive oil. Sprinkle with paprika and chopped parsley and serve.

GUACAMOLE

This delicious invention from Central America is based on the versatile avocado, and can be used as a dip for crudités, corn chips and other crackers (try the Corn Wafers on page 82), or as a sauce for cooked foods.

This is one time I don't use my food processor, because it would make the texture too smooth. You can leave out the chili if you like—or add more!

Makes about 1 cup
1 LARGE, OR 1 ½ SMALL, VERY RIPE AVOCADO(S)
1 cup CHOPPED RIPE TOMATOES
1 GARLIC CLOVE, CRUSHED
2 GREEN ONIONS, FINELY CHOPPED
1 to 2 CHILI PEPPERS, SEEDED AND FINELY CHOPPED (OPTIONAL)
JUICE OF 1 LIME OR LEMON
1 tbl. CHOPPED CILANTRO LEAVES
SALT AND PEPPER
LIME WEDGES AND CILANTRO SPRIGS, TO GARNISH (OPTIONAL)

Peel and seed the avocado(s). Roughly mash the flesh with a fork.

Immediately stir this with all the remaining ingredients. Season to taste with salt and pepper.

Spoon into a serving dish and garnish with lime wedges and cilantro sprigs, if using.

LENTIL AND SUN-DRIED TOMATO PÂTÉ

This tasty pâté couldn't be easier to make, and yet is full of deceptively complex flavors. It is best served with hot toast.

The kind of stock you use will subtly change the flavor—I like to use an onion-based stock cube for this recipe.

Makes about 1 lb.

1 heaping cup of RED LENTILS
3 cups VEGETABLE STOCK (SEE INTRODUCTION)
2 oz. SUN-DRIED TOMATOES IN OIL, DRAINED (ABOUT ⅓ CUP)
SALT AND PEPPER
FRESH TOMATO WEDGES AND SPRIGS OF BASIL, TO GARNISH (OPTIONAL)

Put the lentils and stock in a small saucepan and bring slowly to a boil.

Cover and simmer over as low a heat as possible, undisturbed, until almost all the stock is absorbed. This will take 15 to 20 minutes; watch toward the end to make sure the pan doesn't burn. Remove the lid for the last couple of minutes of cooking time to let any remaining moisture evaporate.

Let the lentils cool. Pour them into the bowl of a food processor or blender. Add the sun-dried tomatoes and process until smooth. Season to taste with salt and pepper.

Spoon the mixture into a serving dish. Garnish with tomato wedges and sprigs of basil, if using.

CLOCKWISE FROM THE BOTTOM LEFT:
Scorched Pepper, Walnut, and Ricotta Pâté (page 24), Corn Wafers (page 82), Lentil and Sun-Dried Tomato Pâté, and Mushroom Pâté (page 24)

EGGPLANT AND SESAME DIP

Use this smoky-tasting paste as a dip, as a spread, or as a filling for pastry shells or stuffed vegetables. Thinned with a little vegetable stock, it may also be used as a sauce for cooked dishes.

Makes about 1 cup
2 EGGPLANTS (TOTAL WEIGHT ABOUT 1 lb.)
1 SMALL MILD ONION, VERY FINELY CHOPPED
2 GARLIC CLOVES, CRUSHED
1 rounded tbl. TAHINI (SEE RECIPE FOR
   HUMMUS ON PAGE 21)
GOOD PINCH OF CHILI POWDER
4 tbl. CHOPPED CILANTRO
SALT AND PEPPER
1 tbl. EXTRA-VIRGIN OLIVE OIL,
   TO DRESS

Preheat the oven to 400°. Bake the eggplants whole for about 15 minutes, or until very soft.

Let the eggplants cool. Scoop out all the flesh and discard the skins.

Mash the flesh well. Mix it together with all the other ingredients except 1 tbl. of the cilantro.

Spoon the dip into a serving dish. Smooth the surface with the back of the spoon and drizzle with the olive oil. Garnish with the reserved cilantro.

SCORCHED PEPPER, WALNUT, AND RICOTTA PÂTÉ

The subtle taste of this creamy pâté contrasts the sweet smoky flavors of the broiled pepper with the earthy taste of walnuts—plus a little added "bite" of horseradish.

Ricotta is a mild-tasting, Italian fresh cheese. It is available from delicatessens and large supermarkets.

Makes about 1 lb.

1 tbl. WALNUT OR OLIVE OIL

2 RED BELL PEPPERS, QUARTERED
    LENGTHWISE AND SEEDED

¾ cup RICOTTA CHEESE

¾ cup FINELY CHOPPED WALNUTS

1 tbl. HORSERADISH SAUCE

JUICE OF ½ LEMON

SALT AND PEPPER

VEGETABLE OIL FOR GREASING

Preheat the broiler on high. Line the broiler pan with foil. Lightly grease the foil with oil.

Arrange the quartered peppers, skin side up, in one layer in the prepared broiler pan. Broil them until all the skins are blackened.

Put the pepper quarters in a plastic bag and let them cook in their own steam for 5 minutes. Peel off the blackened skins over a bowl to catch any juices.

Put the peppers and any juices in the bowl of a food processor or blender with the other ingredients. Add seasoning to taste. Process until smooth.

Transfer the pâté to a serving bowl or plate. Cover and chill for at least 1 hour to let the flavors develop fully.

Scorched Pepper, Walnut, and Ricotta Pâté served with Corn Wafers (page 82)

MUSHROOM PÂTÉ

This succulent pâté will be a huge success with all mushroom lovers. In fact, it has so much flavor that you might have to convince dedicated vegetarians that they aren't actually eating meat. Add a few soaked dried wild mushrooms for an even fuller flavor—and, for very special occasions, garnish with truffles instead of mushrooms!

Serve with hot toast and pickled gherkins or, even better, pickled walnuts.

To clarify butter, simply melt it in a small pan over low heat. Pour it out slowly, leaving the unwanted sediment behind in the pan.

Makes about 1 lb.

1 tbl. EXTRA-VIRGIN OLIVE OIL

1 ONION, FINELY CHOPPED

3 cups FINELY CHOPPED MUSHROOMS (OPEN-
    CAP ONES WILL HAVE THE MOST FLAVOR)

1 GARLIC CLOVE, CRUSHED

2 tbl. FINELY CHOPPED PARSLEY

2 cups CANNED CANNELLINI BEANS, DRAINED
    AND RINSED

SALT AND PEPPER

To garnish

1 BAY LEAF

FEW SMALL THIN SLICES OF
    BUTTON MUSHROOM

2 tbl. CLARIFIED BUTTER
    (SEE INTRODUCTION)

Heat the oil in a small, preferably nonstick, pan. Cook the onion over medium heat for about 5 minutes, or until soft and translucent.

Add the mushrooms, garlic, and parsley and continue to cook, stirring occasionally, for about 10 minutes longer, until they soften and the liquid that comes out of the mushrooms evaporates. Season well with salt and pepper.

Pour the contents of the pan into the bowl of a food processor or blender. Add the drained beans and process to a very smooth purée.

Pack this into an attractive small dish or terrine and make the top as flat and smooth as possible. Garnish by placing the bay leaf in the middle and arrange the mushroom slices around it.

Gently pour the clarified butter over, being careful not to dislodge the garnish. Chill for at least 4 hours, or overnight, to let the flavors develop.

THE MENUS

For a meal to be a complete success it must consist of a well-balanced selection of dishes. In a carnivore's diet, tradition makes this relatively easy for the cook to plan. When designing a vegetarian meal, however, a little more thought is needed to achieve the perfect balance of flavors, textures, and colors.
I have therefore done part of the work for you by grouping the dishes in this book into carefully thought-out menus, each of which serves six people.
Of course, not all of us like the same things. You might hate soup, for instance, or prefer one of your own desserts. These menus are meant only as guidelines, so adapt them as you would season the recipes—to taste.
Happy cooking!

FESTIVE FEASTING

This sophisticated winter menu includes many familiar festive flavors and is designed for Christmas lunch or dinner, or any other special occasion during the holiday season which calls for an elegant, meatless meal.

SALAD OF RED AND GREEN LEAVES WITH FETA, WALNUTS, AND MOSTARDA FRUITS

CHESTNUT, APPLE, AND ONION PIE
CUMBERLAND SAUCE
HUNGARIAN BRAISED RED CABBAGE
CHOPSTICK POTATOES

PLUM PUDDING ICE CREAM

SALAD OF RED AND GREEN LEAVES WITH FETA, WALNUTS, AND MOSTARDA FRUITS

This is my favorite salad of the moment and is good at any time of the year. Yet somehow it fits the bill perfectly as a festive first course, particularly at Christmas, with its combination of red and green leaves and the glistening jewel-like mostarda fruits looking like decorations on the tree.

Mostarda fruits are an unusual and delicious Italian preserve made from crystallized fruits in a heavy mustard-flavored syrup. Traditionally eaten in Italy with hot and cold meats of all kinds, they are incredibly versatile and have many uses for non-meat-eaters, too! They are available in jars from gourmet food stores and Italian grocery stores. Also available in these stores is balsamic vinegar, made in Modena from grape juice concentrate and aged for 15 to 20 years in wooden casks to give it a dark, sweet-and-sour taste.

14 oz. **ITALIAN MOSTARDA FRUITS (SEE INTRODUCTION)**

8 oz. **MIXED RED AND GREEN LEAVES**

3 tbl. **OLIVE OIL**

2 **GARLIC CLOVES, THINLY SLICED**

3 oz. **WHITE BREAD, CUT INTO ½-inch CUBES** (about 1½ cups)

1 cup **SHELLED WALNUTS**

1½ cups **FETA CHEESE, CUT INTO ½-inch CUBES**

For the dressing

1 tbl. **BALSAMIC VINEGAR**

3 tbl. **EXTRA-VIRGIN OLIVE OIL**

SALT AND PEPPER

Drain the mostarda fruits, reserving 1 tbl. of the syrup. Remove any pits and roughly chop the fruits.

Arrange the leaves decoratively on 6 large plates.

In a wok or skillet, heat the oil over low to medium heat. Stir-fry the garlic and bread cubes until the bread is golden and crispy. Discard the garlic and drain the croutons on paper towels.

To make the dressing, place all the ingredients in a small screw-top jar. Add the reserved syrup. Seal the jar and shake together until the ingredients are amalgamated.

Sprinkle the croutons, walnut pieces, cheese, and mostarda fruits over the leaves. Drizzle with the dressing. Serve immediately.

CHESTNUT, APPLE, AND ONION PIE

This unusual pie is loosely based on a traditional recipe from the gloriously wild hills of the Cévennes in southern France. There chestnuts were once the main crop and were relied on as a staple by the poor country folk, who thought up every imaginable way of using them in both sweet and savory dishes. The original recipe contained some pork, but this version is just as tasty.

Cooking and peeling chestnuts is, I am afraid, a bore. They are best roasted, but you can also boil them. If you simply can't face the effort, use canned whole chestnuts. Making the rest of the pie is simplicity itself.

1¼ lbs. **BASIC PIECRUST DOUGH (SEE PAGE 18)**

For the filling

2 tbl. **OLIVE OIL**

2½ cups **CHOPPED ONIONS**

1 lb. **DESSERT APPLES (ABOUT 3), PEELED AND CORED**

10 TO 11 **COOKED AND PEELED CHESTNUTS (SEE INTRODUCTION)**

1 tsp. **CHOPPED FRESH THYME OR** ½ tsp. **DRIED**

1 tsp. **CHOPPED FRESH SAGE OR** ½ tsp. **DRIED**

3 **EGGS**

SALT AND PEPPER

MILK FOR GLAZING

Preheat the oven to 400°.

Heat the oil in a sauté pan or skillet over medium heat. Add the onions and cook until they are golden brown.

Meanwhile, chop the apples into ¼-inch dice; don't use the food processor, or you might end up with a mush. Put these into a large bowl and add the onions.

Cut the chestnuts into quarters. Add them and the herbs to the bowl. Season well and mix together.

Beat 2 of the eggs. Add these to the bowl and stir together.

Roll out two-thirds of the dough and use it to line the bottom of a nonstick, loose-bottomed fluted 9½-inch tart pan. Spoon in the chestnut mixture, smoothing it into a mound shape.

Roll out the remaining dough to make a lid. Place on top of the pie, trim off the excess, and seal the edges with a little water. Decorate the top of the pie with dough trimmings.

Beat the remaining egg with a little milk and use some of this to glaze the pie.

Bake for 40 to 50 minutes or until golden brown. If you like, 10 minutes before the pie is cooked, carefully remove the sides of the pan, brush the sides of the pie with the remaining egg glaze, and return to the oven to brown the sides.

Serve hot with Cumberland Sauce (see page 20).

HUNGARIAN BRAISED RED CABBAGE

The original Hungarian recipe for this succulent fragrant dish uses goose fat or lard, but this version uses olive oil and tastes even better.

1 tbl. OLIVE OIL

1 ONION, CHOPPED

10 cups FINELY SHREDDED RED CABBAGE

5 cups FINELY SHREDDED WHITE CABBAGE

3 tbl. WHITE-WINE VINEGAR OR CIDER
    VINEGAR

2 tbl. SUGAR

1 BAY LEAF

SALT AND PEPPER

2 cups VEGETABLE STOCK

In a large saucepan which has a lid, heat the oil over medium heat. Cook the onion in the oil until it is golden.

Add the remaining ingredients and stir together.

Bring to a boil. Cover and simmer for about 30 minutes, or until the cabbage is tender.

CHOPSTICK POTATOES

These are really simply a variation of classic roasted potatoes, which need not be taboo to vegetarians just because they are traditionally cooked around a roast, or in meat fat in a separate pan. Roasted potatoes cooked in olive oil are even tastier, and this "chopstick" slicing method not only makes for an unusual and attractive presentation, but means the potatoes end up with more crispy outside bits! If you are cooking these in the oven with the pie, they will need to go in 10 to 15 minutes before it does.

3 tbl. EXTRA-VIRGIN OLIVE OIL

9 EVENLY SHAPED MEDIUM BAKING POTATOES
    (ABOUT 3 lbs. IN TOTAL)

KOSHER SALT

PEPPER

Preheat the oven to 400°. Grease a roasting pan with 1 tbl. of the oil.

Peel the potatoes and cut them in half lengthwise. Cook in boiling salted water for 5 minutes; drain.

Place each potato half, cut side down, horizontally on a chopping board. Place a chopstick running along the top and bottom of each potato half as you get ready to cut it.

Using a sharp knife, make vertical cuts across the potato about ¼ inch apart. (The chopsticks will prevent the knife from cutting right through the potato.)

Arrange the potato ''chopsticks'' in the prepared baking pan. Drizzle with the remaining oil, letting it seep into the slits.

Roast for about 1 hour (see introduction), or until crisp and golden. Baste the potatoes a couple of times during the process. Sprinkle them with kosher salt and pepper about 15 minutes before the end of cooking.

PLUM PUDDING ICE CREAM

This is a wonderfully simple idea from Australia, where they celebrate Christmas in the middle of summer. It makes a pleasant change from the somewhat heavier plum pudding with hard sauce—although it is still hardly food for weight-watchers!

Vegetarians must be careful when buying imported British Christmas puddings, as many contain beef suet. Read the ingredients label carefully. The easiest solution, however, is to make your own from a classic recipe and substitute grated frozen butter for the suet.

In American cookbooks look for a recipe for plum pudding, but in British cookbooks you'll find the same steamed dessert called a "Christmas pudding." If you visit Britain, vegetarian suet is sold in supermarkets and will keep almost indefinitely until you are ready to make this pudding.

Another suitable alternative is to substitute crumbled moist fruit cake for the plum pudding in this recipe—preferably one that contains plenty of brandy or rum!

1 pint BEST-QUALITY VANILLA ICE CREAM
8 oz. PLUM PUDDING (SEE INTRODUCTION),
    MASHED OR FINELY CRUMBLED

Soften the ice cream slightly by removing it from the freezer for 10 to 15 minutes.

Pour the softened ice cream into a bowl. Quickly but thoroughly stir in the crumbled plum pudding.

Return the mixture to the freezer proof container. Freeze to firm it up.

PARTY FINGER FOOD

Bite size and beautiful, this collection of delicious nibbles makes a perfect cocktail-party menu for any time of the year. Allow six to eight "bites" per guest.

DEEP-FRIED CAMEMBERT-STUFFED OLIVES

STUFFED GRAPE LEAVES

MINI "PIZZAS"

CRUDITÉS WITH DIPS

BÖREKS WITH SPINACH AND RICOTTA

TEENY-WEENY "BLINIS"

DEEP-FRIED CAMEMBERT-STUFFED OLIVES

These are much easier to make than they sound and are absolutely delicious, so do try them. However, if you can't get anyone else to do the last-minute frying for you, don't forget to put an apron over your best dress—not only to guard it from splashed fat, but to ensure that you don't rejoin your guests smelling like a short-order cafeteria!

If you don't own a cherry or olive pitter, invest in one—or don't even attempt this recipe!

Makes 24

24 OF THE BIGGEST RIPE OLIVES YOU CAN FIND
2 oz. CAMEMBERT CHEESE
1 EGG, BEATEN
4 tbl. FINE BREAD CRUMBS
ALL-PURPOSE FLOUR FOR DUSTING
VEGETABLE OIL FOR DEEP-FRYING

Pit the olives. Stuff the resulting cavities with little pieces of the Camembert cheese.

Put the flour, beaten egg, and bread crumbs into 3 separate bowls.

Dip the stuffed olives first in the flour, then in the beaten egg, and then finally in the bread crumbs.

Heat the oil until just smoking. Deep-fry the coated olives for a couple of minutes, until golden brown and crisp.

Drain for a few seconds on paper towels. Serve immediately.

STUFFED GRAPE LEAVES

Versions of these nibbles are served all over Greece, Turkey, and the Middle East as part of the premeal mezze or as snacks.

If you are lucky enough to have fresh grape leaves, boil them for 5 minutes in salted water, then drain and refresh them in cold water before use. Preserved grape leaves are available in plastic packages or cans from delicatessens and supermarkets. Prepare them for use according to the package directions. Either type of leaf should be thoroughly dried on dish towels or paper towels.

The stuffed grape leaves are nice served with yogurt as a dip.

4 tbl. EXTRA-VIRGIN OLIVE OIL
1 LARGE ONION, CHOPPED
⅔ cup BASMATI RICE, RINSED AND DRIED
⅓ cup DRIED CURRANTS
⅓ cup PINE NUTS
2 tbl. CHOPPED MINT, DILL, OR PARSLEY (IN THAT ORDER OF PREFERENCE)
1 cup VEGETABLE STOCK
1 tsp. SALT
8 oz. GRAPE LEAVES (SEE INTRODUCTION)
JUICE OF 1 LEMON
PEPPER

Heat half the oil in a small to medium heavy-bottomed saucepan over medium heat. Cook the onion, stirring occasionally, for about 5 minutes, or until soft and translucent.

Add the rice and stir until each grain is coated with oil. Cover and cook over the lowest possible heat, stirring occasionally, for 5 minutes longer.

Add the fruit, nuts, herbs, stock, salt, and a couple of good grinds of pepper. Simmer, uncovered, for about 5 minutes, or until all the liquid has been absorbed.

Place the grape leaves shiny side down. Put about 1 heaped tsp. of the rice mixture in the middle of each. Working with one leaf at a time, fold the stem end, then fold in the sides. Roll it up into a neat bundle; do not roll them too tightly because the rice swells while the bundles cook. Continue until you have used up all the leaves or all the filling. (The number that you make will depend on the size of the leaves.)

Arrange the rolls, seam side down, in a large pan which has a lid, in layers if necessary. (I use a sauté pan.)

Drizzle with the remaining olive oil and the lemon juice. Add just enough hot water barely to cover the rolls. Place a heatproof plate on top of the rolls to stop them jiggling about and coming undone while they cook.

Cover the pan and cook over the lowest possible heat for 1 hour. Check halfway through to make sure that the liquid hasn't evaporated; add a little more if necessary.

Remove the pan from the heat. Let the stuffed grape leaves cool in the liquid. Drain and arrange on a plate.

MINI "PIZZAS"

These mouthwatering little bites are made not with bread dough, but with commercial frozen puff pastry dough. One 13- to 14-oz. package will make about 48 of these. This may sound like a lot, but they will disappear in minutes.

Makes 48

Preheat the oven to 425°.

Roll out the thawed dough as thinly as possible. Stamp out bite-sized circles using a small cookie cutter or the rim of a small glass.

Add the toppings of choice (see below). Bake for 7 to 10 minutes.

Suggestions for toppings: try olive paste and pesto (from delicatessens); slivers of mozzarella cheese, chèvre, and other well-flavored cheeses; slivers of sun-dried tomatoes; slices of small ripe olives, pieces of scorched pepper (see page 24), small chunks of avocado (delicious hot!)—the possibilities are endless.

CRUDITÉS WITH DIPS

In France I often choose a simple plate of "crudités" as a first course. However, what arrives on the table will not be the same as the raw, unadorned "crudités" which have become the universal healthy and popular snack and party food. In France they will consist of an assortment of dressed vegetable salads. Oddly enough, moreover, a good proportion of these vegetables might be cooked—not raw—like beets or even asparagus in season.

For this menu, however, I suggest serving a selection of raw vegetables, cut into manageable bite-sized (or two-bite-sized) pieces, which are convenient for scooping up a variety of thick dressings or dips. As big a selection as possible looks impressive and attractive.

Choose from: green onions, celery, bell peppers, carrots, radishes, broccoli and cauliflower flowerets, crunchy cabbage strips, snow peas, and sugar-snap peas.

When in season, nothing is more delicious raw than fresh peas or young fava beans. Just remove them from their shells and either offer them in little bowls to be eaten like peanuts, or thread bite-sized rows of them on toothpicks to be "dipped."

Choose a selection of dips from the Breads and Basics chapter, beginning on page 21.

BÖREKS WITH SPINACH AND RICOTTA

These mouthwatering little phyllo pastry bundles are much quicker and easier to make than you might imagine. Once you have learned the knack of folding the dough you can experiment with your own fillings.

Phyllo pastry dough is available frozen from supermarkets and occasionally fresh from delicatessens; you will often find it labelled "filo." It dries out and becomes brittle very quickly so you must work with only one sheet at a time. Re-roll the rest of the sheets each time you remove one, and cover the roll with plastic wrap and a slightly damp dish towel.

6 tbl. BUTTER, MELTED
2 tbl. OLIVE OIL
1 SMALL ONION, FINELY CHOPPED
4 cups FINELY CHOPPED, RINSED AND THOROUGHLY DRIED SPINACH
½ cup RICOTTA CHEESE
1 EGG
½ tbl. PINE NUTS
6 SHEETS OF PHYLLO PASTRY DOUGH (SEE INTRODUCTION), DEFROSTED IF FROZEN
SALT AND PEPPER

Preheat the oven to 350°. Grease a baking sheet with a little of the butter.

Heat the oil in a pan over medium heat. Cook the onion, stirring, for about 5 minutes, or until soft and translucent.

Add the spinach and continue to cook, stirring constantly, for 2 to 3 minutes longer, or until it just begins to wilt; do not overcook or the spinach will turn to a mush.

Transfer the contents of the pan to a bowl and let cool.

In another bowl, mash the cheese with a fork. Stir in the egg and beat together until smooth. Season well with salt and pepper.

Stir in the pine nuts and the spinach mixture. (The filling doesn't look like much at this stage but do not worry.)

Lay one sheet of phyllo pastry dough (see introduction) on a counter with the long edges running away from you. Brush it all over with melted butter.

Cut the dough lengthwise into 4 equal long strips. Place a heaped tsp. of the filling on each of the ends closest to you.

Working with one strip at a time, fold one edge diagonally over the filling to make a triangle, bringing the corner up to meet the opposite side. Continue folding up the length of the dough strip in this manner to make a neat, triangular bundle.

As each bundle is made, arrange it seam side down, on the prepared baking sheet. Continue until all the dough and all the filling are used. Brush the tops of the bundles with the remaining butter. Bake for 40 to 45 minutes, or until crisp and golden. Serve immediately.

TEENY-WEENY ''BLINIS''

Although Russian in inspiration, my versions of these little pancakes are far from authentic because they are leavened with baking powder instead of yeast. This makes them much quicker and easier—and just as nice, I think.

You can top these with whatever you like: a dollop of cream cheese, fromage frais, or yogurt is good garnished with chopped hard-boiled egg, onion, gherkins, capers, or other pickles. Alternatively, try any of the pâtés or dips on pages 21 to 24 in the Breads and Basics chapter, topped with fresh herbs or other suitable garnishes.

Makes 48

2 cups ALL-PURPOSE FLOUR

heaped 2 tsp. BAKING POWDER

1 tsp. SALT

1 cup MILK

2 EGGS, BEATEN

PEPPER

VEGETABLE OIL FOR FRYING

TOPPINGS OF CHOICE (SEE INTRODUCTION)

In a bowl, mix together the flour, baking powder, and salt. Season with a few twists of pepper. Add the milk and eggs and beat to make a smooth batter.

Lightly oil a skillet and place it over medium heat. When hot, drop teaspoonfuls of batter into the pan, about 4 at a time.

Cook the blinis for 2 to 3 minutes, turning them over once, or until cooked through and golden brown on each side.

If you want to serve them hot, keep them warm in a covered dish in a slow (275°) oven while cooking the remaining batches. However, I generally serve them cool because it is less of a last-minute bother. Any extras freeze well.

Add toppings of your choice and serve.

BEAUTIFUL BREAKFASTS

Make time occasionally to prepare a really special breakfast, and remember there is life beyond bacon and eggs or croissants and coffee. So invite friends over on Sunday for a lazy, convivial morning complete with mouthwatering food and the papers.

PASSION FRUIT MUFFINS WITH PRESERVES

BANANA BREAD FRENCH TOAST WITH DRIED FRUIT COMPOTE

POACHED EGGS ON POTATO CAKES WITH HOLLANDAISE SAUCE

FROMAGE FRAIS WITH MELON PURÉE

PASSION FRUIT MUFFINS WITH PRESERVES

Like most muffins, these are best eaten warm straight from the oven. As they take only minutes to prepare, they are ideal for special breakfasts and make a refreshing change from croissants or brioche.

3 tbl. BUTTER, MELTED, PLUS MORE FOR
   GREASING
2¼ cups ALL-PURPOSE FLOUR, SIFTED
1 rounded tbl. BAKING POWDER
½ tsp. SALT
1 tbl. SUGAR
JUICE AND PULP OF 4
   PASSION FRUIT
1 cup MILK
1 EGG, LIGHTLY BEATEN
To serve
BUTTER, FROMAGE FRAIS (SEE PAGE 41),
   YOGURT, OR SOUR CREAM
JAMS OR PRESERVES, OR MORE
   PASSION FRUIT

Preheat the oven to 425°. Butter a 12-cup muffin pan.

In one large bowl, mix the flour, baking powder, salt, and sugar together. In another bowl, or in a measuring jug, beat together the remaining ingredients.

Pour the liquid ingredients into the dry ones and mix together quickly just until the flour is moistened—but do not beat the batter!

Divide the batter between the prepared muffin cups. Bake for 20 to 25 minutes, until well risen and a toothpick inserted into the middle of a muffin comes out clean.

Set the muffins onto a wire rack. Let them cool for 1 to 2 minutes, then serve warm. (Any leftover muffins are also nice cold.)

Serve the muffins with butter and jams or preserves, or perhaps a dish of fromage frais, yogurt, or sour cream, with the juice and pulp of a couple of passion fruit spooned over the top.

BANANA BREAD FRENCH TOAST WITH DRIED FRUIT COMPOTE

This is a wonderfully satisfying fruity breakfast dish. The bread and the compote can be made the day before.

3 EGGS, LIGHTLY BEATEN
6 tbl. MILK
6 SLICES OF BANANA BREAD (SEE
   PAGE 17), ABOUT ½-inch THICK
6 tbl. BUTTER
6 tbl. CRÈME FRAÎCHE (SEE PAGE 47) OR
   YOGURT, TO SERVE (OPTIONAL)
For the compote
2¼ cups PRUNES
2¼ cups NO-SOAK DRIED APRICOTS
2 cups ORANGE JUICE (IF FROM A CARTON, USE
   THE PURE UNSWEETENED KIND)
3 tbl. CHUNKY ORANGE MARMALADE

The day before, make the compote. Place all the ingredients in a heavy-bottomed pan which has a tight-fitting lid. Bring to a boil. Turn down the heat, cover, and simmer for 30 minutes, stirring occasionally. Let cool.

On the next day, beat the eggs and milk together in a shallow dish or soup plate. Dip the slices of banana bread in it until they are thoroughly soaked on both sides.

Melt the butter in a skillet over low to medium heat. Cook the slices of bread in it until they are brown on both sides. Drain for a few seconds on paper towels, then cut each slice of bread in half.

While the bread is frying, reheat the compote slowly.

Arrange the slices of ''French toast'' on 6 warmed plates. Top with some of the fruit compote and crème fraîche or yogurt, if using.

POACHED EGGS ON POTATO CAKES WITH HOLLANDAISE SAUCE

There are lots of recipes for old-fashioned potato cakes, but this is my own version which is "spiked" with chopped green onion.

Many people find poaching eggs very difficult, because the eggs tend to spread in a messy fashion when they are dropped into the water. The secret is to use the freshest of eggs. A drop of vinegar in the water also helps, but do not add salt as this encourages the egg white to break up and defeats the purpose. (This is why you do add a pinch of salt when beating egg whites.)

2¼ cups MASHED POTATOES (MADE FROM ABOUT 1½ lbs. UNCOOKED POTATOES)
2 GREEN ONIONS, TRIMMED AND FINELY CHOPPED
7 VERY FRESH EGGS
½ tsp. SALT
1 cup ALL-PURPOSE FLOUR
1 tsp. BAKING POWDER
1 tsp. VINEGAR
about ⅔ cup HOLLANDAISE SAUCE (SEE PAGE 20)
PEPPER
VEGETABLE OIL FOR FRYING

In a large bowl, mix together the mashed potatoes, green onions, one of the eggs (lightly beaten), the salt, and a good twist of black pepper.

Combine the flour and baking powder. Add enough of the flour mixture, holding a little back, to make a not-too-sticky dough with the consistency of a biscuit dough. If it is too moist, add a little more of the flour mixture.

Roll out the dough about ½ inch thick. Use a 3½-inch round cookie cutter to cut out 6 cakes, rerolling the trimmings if necessary.

Heat a little oil in a skillet over low heat. Fry the potato cakes for about 5 minutes on each side, until golden brown and cooked through. The outsides should be crispy, but the insides will still be soft and a bit mushy. Keep them warm.

Meanwhile, fill another skillet three-quarters full with water and add the vinegar. Bring just to a simmer over low heat. Working in batches of no more than 2 eggs at a time, poach the remaining eggs by dropping them into the water.

As soon as the eggs are cooked to taste, remove them from the pan with a pancake turner. Drain them well and keep them warm in a covered dish while cooking the rest.

Place a hot potato cake on each plate. Top each with a poached egg. Pour on some warm Hollandaise Sauce and serve immediately.

FROMAGE FRAIS WITH MELON PURÉE

Fromage frais is a delicious, bland-tasting fresh cheese which has always been popular in France but has recently caught on in other countries. Available from specialist gourmet food stores, it comes with varying fat contents—even the no-fat version tastes wonderfully creamy.

The mild flavor of fromage frais makes it incredibly versatile in the kitchen. As well as being used in cooking, it can be eaten just as it is as an alternative to cream cheese, used as a base for dips and sauces, or served with fresh fruit, fruit sauces, and purées for breakfast or desserts.

Look for fromage frais in the dairy section of gourmet food stores. If you can't find any, beat together equal quantities of light cream cheese and plain yogurt to make a suitable alternative.

4 cups CHOPPED MELON FLESH (1 MEDIUM MELON SHOULD SUFFICE)
1 tsp. GROUND GINGER
2 cups FROMAGE FRAIS
CHOPPED PRESERVED GINGER, FRESH MINT, LEMON BALM LEAVES, OR EDIBLE FLOWERS, TO GARNISH (OPTIONAL)

Purée the melon flesh and the ginger in a food processor or blender. Chill the purée for at least 2 hours, or preferably overnight.

Divide the fromage frais between 6 dishes or bowls (glass looks nice) and spoon the melon purée over. Garnish with the chopped ginger, leaves or flowers, if using.

ALFRESCO FARE

This menu is designed for outdoor entertaining, with all the dishes easily prepared in advance to be served cool. It is always fun to entertain "alfresco," whether it be simply on a table in the back yard or the perfect picnic at an outdoor music concert.

**GOLDEN MUSHROOM CREAM TART
CHEESE, ONION, AND CORN TART**

**SALADE RUSSE
BEETS WITH SOUR CREAM AND
HERBS
GREEK SALAD**

**CHOCOLATE BROWNIES WITH
HONEYED CRÈME FRAÎCHE AND
BERRIES**

GOLDEN MUSHROOM CREAM TART

This recipe was given to me by Ursula Ferrigno, a brilliant and innovative vegetarian cook in London. Ursula is Italian by descent and specializes in teaching regional Italian vegetarian dishes, the list of which is endless. After all, Italians very often cook and enjoy vegetable-based dishes whether or not they are vegetarian.

I always imagined that I didn't like whole-wheat pastry—as it is so often hard, heavy, and tasteless—until I tried this recipe, which produces light crispy, crumbly, and buttery results.

For the tart shell
1 cup WHOLE-WHEAT FLOUR
1 tsp. BAKING POWDER
GOOD PINCH OF SALT
1 tsp. BROWN SUGAR
4 tbl. BUTTER
2 tsp. OLIVE OIL
For the filling
4 tbl. OLIVE OIL
1 WHOLE HEAD OF GARLIC, CLOVES
   PEELED BUT LEFT WHOLE
2 ONIONS, CHOPPED
1 tbl. CHOPPED PARSLEY
¼ tsp. PAPRIKA
2 tbl. BUTTER
3 cups SLICED MUSHROOMS
4 tbl. PLAIN YOGURT OR FROMAGE FRAIS
   (see p. 41)
1 EGG, BEATEN
SALT AND PEPPER

First make the dough. Put the dry ingredients in a bowl. Cut in the butter until the mixture resembles fine bread crumbs. Stir in 3 tbl. of cold water and the oil until a dough forms. (I make mine in a food processor.) Chill for at least 30 minutes.

Roll out the chilled dough and use to line a 9-inch loose-bottomed tart pan. Chill until required.

Now make the filling. Heat half the oil in a small, heavy-bottomed saucepan over medium heat. Sauté the garlic cloves for 3 minutes, stirring frequently.

Add 1¼ cups water and salt and pepper to taste. Cover and simmer for 45 minutes. Purée the contents of the saucepan in a food processor or blender.

Preheat the oven to 400°.

Heat the remaining oil in a heavy-bottomed pan which has a lid over very low heat. Sauté the onions and parsley, stirring frequently, for 10 minutes.

Cover the pan and simmer for 15 minutes longer, stirring occasionally. Stir in the paprika, salt and pepper, and garlic purée. Cook this over high heat, stirring, for 2 to 3 minutes, until reduced to a thick, creamy sauce.

Melt the butter in a skillet over medium heat. Stir-fry the mushrooms for 5 to 10 minutes, or until completely soft. Season with salt and pepper and stir in 1 tbl. of the yogurt or fromage frais.

Mix the remaining yogurt or fromage frais with the beaten egg and season with salt and pepper.

Bake the pastry shell empty for 5 minutes. Spread the mushroom mixture over the bottom of the shell. Cover this with the onion and garlic sauce and pour the egg mixture over. Return the tart to the oven and bake for 20 minutes.

Serve hot, warm, or cool.

CHEESE, ONION, AND CORN TART

The filling for this old-fashioned tart is less rich than a classic quiche filling, using fewer eggs and milk instead of cream. Nevertheless, it is creamy in texture and savory tasting—and costs considerably less to make!

This quantity will provide 6 slices as part of a buffet, but makes 4 good main-course helpings.

8 oz. BASIC PIECRUST DOUGH (SEE PAGE 18)
4 tbl. BUTTER
2 LARGE ONIONS, CHOPPED
1 tsp. DRY MUSTARD
1 rounded tbl. ALL-PURPOSE FLOUR
1¼ cups MILK
½ cup GRATED CHEDDAR OR OTHER TASTY
   HARD CHEESE
1 EGG, LIGHTLY BEATEN
¾ cup WHOLE-KERNEL CORN, DRAINED IF
   CANNED OR DEFROSTED IF FROZEN
SALT AND PEPPER

Preheat the oven to 400°.

Roll out the dough and use it to line a 9-inch loose-bottomed tart pan. Chill while making the filling.

Melt the butter in a saucepan over medium heat. Cook the onions for 5 to 10 minutes, stirring constantly, until soft and golden.

Add the mustard and flour and stir together. Stir in the milk and bring to a boil, stirring constantly. Turn down the heat and simmer for 2 to 3 minutes.

Stir in the cheese. Remove the pan from the heat and let the mixture cool for 2 to 3 minutes. Stir in the egg and corn and season with salt and pepper.

Pour the filling into the tart shell. Bake for 30 to 40 minutes, or until the filling is set and the top golden. Serve hot, warm, or cool.

SALADE RUSSE

The mere thought of Russian salad used to conjure up childhood memories of something horrid out of a can which appeared on "plate salads," until I read four short lines while browsing through a Victorian cookbook I found in a junk shop in Australia. Reading the description of Russian salad on page 87 of the Berrambool Cookbook by a certain Mrs. Alured Kelly, I realized that, homemade, it could be no less than delicious—and thoroughly deserves a revival. Here are Mrs. Kelly's directions:

"Ingredients: peas, French (green) beans, carrots, asparagus, small potatoes in equal quantities all nicely cooked. Mix well with mayonnaise sauce."

BEETS WITH SOUR CREAM AND HERBS

This quick-and-easy salad with a difference is special enough to serve as a cold first course. It looks stunning, with the bright green of the fresh herbs against the pinks and purples of the beets. Use whatever herbs are available, such as parsley, dill, chives, tarragon, cilantro, basil, or marjoram.

1½ cups DICED COOKED BEETS
3 rounded tbl. SOUR CREAM OR PLAIN YOGURT
2 tbl. CHOPPED FRESH HERBS
    (SEE ABOVE)
SALT AND PEPPER

Put the beets in a bowl. Stir in the sour cream or yogurt. Season with salt and pepper.

Transfer to a serving dish and sprinkle with herbs. Serve at room temperature or chilled.

GREEK SALAD

Anyone who has been to Greece in the summer will be very familiar with this filling savory salad. To me, it is one of the few foreign dishes that tastes better at home!

After being served this at almost every meal on a small Greek island one summer I began to hate it. Once back home, however, I soon started to prepare it myself to remind me of the brilliant blue sky and sea and the dazzling whitewashed houses of the Aegean.

This really is a summer salad, so it is simply not worth bothering to make it unless you can get really ripe tasty tomatoes.

If you make the salad in advance and keep it in the refrigerator, take it out at least 30 minutes before serving because it tastes much better at room temperature. If you want to serve this as a substantial main course, simply double the quantities.

8 oz. TOMATOES, SLICED, ROUGHLY CHOPPED,
    OR CUT INTO SMALL WEDGES
1⅓ cups ROUGHLY CHOPPED OR CRUMBLED
    FETA CHEESE
½ CUCUMBER, SLICED OR CUT INTO
    BITE-SIZE CHUNKS
1 MILD ONION, SLICED
1 RED, GREEN, OR YELLOW BELL PEPPER,
    SEEDED AND CHOPPED (OPTIONAL)
½ cup RIPE OLIVES
3 tbl. FRUITY EXTRA-VIRGIN
    OLIVE OIL
SALT AND PEPPER
6 LEMON WEDGES, TO SERVE

Place the tomatoes, cheese, cucumber, onion, pepper if using, and the olives in a bowl. Season with salt and pepper. Pour the oil over. Toss together.

Arrange the lemon slices on top of the salad. Each person squeezes her or his own lemon juice over the salad.

CHOCOLATE BROWNIES WITH HONEYED CRÈME FRAÎCHE AND BERRIES

There are endless variations on recipes for chocolate brownies: some are sticky and fudgy, some are more spongy; some have nuts, some have fruit; some are iced and some are not. This version is light and spongy, with a few walnut pieces for crunch. It makes a good plain cake for a packed lunch, or may be served as it is here, as a luxurious dessert to round off a special menu.

Crème fraîche is available in delicatessens and some specialty supermarkets. If you can't find any, substitute sour cream or heavy cream.

½ cup UNSALTED BUTTER, PLUS MORE FOR GREASING

1 cup ALL-PURPOSE FLOUR, PLUS MORE FOR COATING

3½ oz. SEMISWEET CHOCOLATE, MELTED

¼ tsp. BAKING SODA

¼ tsp. SALT

½ heaping cup of SUGAR

2 JUMBO EGGS

½ tsp. VANILLA EXTRACT

3 tbl. MILK

½ cup CHOPPED WALNUTS

To serve

⅔ cup CRÈME FRAÎCHE (SEE ABOVE)

1 tbl. HONEY

12 oz. BERRIES OR OTHER FRESH FRUIT IN SEASON

Preheat the oven to 350°. Grease an 8-inch square cake pan with butter and coat it with flour.

Melt the chocolate in a heatproof bowl set over a pan of simmering water (or in a microwave). Remove from the heat and let cool.

Sift the flour, baking soda, and the salt together onto a sheet of waxed paper.

In a bowl, cream the butter and sugar until light and fluffy. (I use an electric mixer.) Beat in the eggs, one at a time, followed by the vanilla. Beat together, then beat in the cooled melted chocolate.

Beat in alternating thirds of the sifted flour mixture and the milk. Stir in the chopped nuts.

Pour the batter into the prepared pan. Bake for 30 to 35 minutes, or until a toothpick inserted into the middle comes out clean.

Run a spatula around the edge of the pan. Turn out the cake onto a wire rack to cool. When cool, cut it into 6 equal portions.

To serve, place a piece of brownie on each plate. Whip the cream with the honey, then spoon this over or alongside the brownie. Add some fruit.

AN INTERNATIONAL AFFAIR

This eclectic dinner-party menu brings together inspiration from France, Italy, the U.S.A., and Australia to produce a memorable meal that will impress any guest—however sophisticated and well-traveled—without your having to spend hours in the kitchen.

FRENCH ONION SOUP

CABBAGE GÂTEAU
SWEET POTATO HASH
CARROTS BRAISED IN OLIVE OIL
WITH ROSEMARY AND GARLIC

FRESH PEACH PAVLOVA

FRENCH ONION SOUP

This well-loved classic is perhaps most famous for having been enjoyed in the small hours by night revelers and market porters alike in the Paris cafés which surrounded the vegetable market of Les Halles.

The authentic way to serve this homey and comforting soup is to place the bread and cheese in the bottom of each bowl before pouring in the hot soup. I prefer my bread less soggy and like to float it on top. I also prefer the taste of the cheese when broiled.

4 tbl. BUTTER
1 tbl. VEGETABLE OIL
4½ cups THINLY SLICED ONIONS
1 rounded tbl. ALL-PURPOSE FLOUR
1½ quarts VEGETABLE STOCK
6 SLICES OF FRENCH BREAD
½ cup GRATED SWISS OR GRUYÈRE CHEESE
SALT AND PEPPER

In a large saucepan, melt the butter with the oil over very low heat. Cook the onions, stirring occasionally, for 20 to 30 minutes, or until soft and brown but not burned.

Add the flour, stir well, and cook for 1 minute longer.

Stir in the stock, cover, and simmer for 20 minutes. Season to taste.

While the soup is simmering, preheat a hot broiler.

Just before serving, broil the French bread slices lightly on both sides. Top one side of each with grated cheese. Return them to the broiler and broil until the cheese bubbles.

Pour the soup into warm bowls and float one of the cheese toasts on top of each bowl. Serve immediately.

CABBAGE GÂTEAU

Though quick and easy to make, the spectacular appearance of this savory "cake" makes it perfect for a special dinner party.

If you can't find fresh dill, substitute the same quantity of tarragon, parsley, chervil, or chives. If you don't have any pine nuts, substitute chopped walnuts, peanuts, or cashew nuts.

3 tbl. OLIVE OIL, PLUS MORE FOR GREASING
2½ cups FINELY CHOPPED CABBAGE (ANY KIND), PLUS 6 LARGE LEAVES
2 ONIONS, CHOPPED
3 GARLIC CLOVES, CRUSHED
3 cups CHOPPED MUSHROOMS
1 heaping cup of EGGPLANT, COARSELY CHOPPED INTO ¼-INCH DICE
⅓ cup PINE NUTS (SEE INTRODUCTION)
2 cups FRESH BREAD CRUMBS (WHOLE-WHEAT OR WHITE)
SALT AND PEPPER
3 EGGS
1 cup RICOTTA CHEESE
1 tbl. FINELY CHOPPED FRESH DILL (SEE INTRODUCTION)

Preheat the oven to 400°. Grease an 8-inch round cake pan with a little oil.

Blanch the large whole cabbage leaves in a large pan of boiling salted water for 5 minutes. Drain them, then plunge them into a bowl of very cold water to refresh them. Drain and pat dry on dish towels or paper towels.

Using a sharp knife, horizontally slice the thick central stem of each cabbage leaf level with the leaf; do not cut out the whole stem. Line the bottom and sides of the prepared cake pan with the cabbage leaves, leaving enough of each sticking above the rim of the pan to fold over and cover the filling.

LEFT TO RIGHT: *French Onion Soup, Cabbage Gâteau, and Carrots Braised in Olive Oil with Rosemary and Garlic*

Heat the oil in a heavy-bottomed saucepan over medium heat. Cook the onion, garlic, and mushrooms, stirring frequently, for 10 to 15 minutes, or until soft. Pour the contents of the pan into a bowl. Stir in the chopped cabbage, eggplant, pine nuts and bread crumbs. Season well with salt and pepper.

Let this cool for 1 or 2 minutes. Beat 2 of the eggs and blend them into the filling mixture.

In another bowl, beat the cheese with the remaining egg and the herbs. (I do this in a food processor.) Season with salt and pepper.

Pack half the cabbage mixture into the lined cake pan. Smooth the ricotta mixture over this to make a middle layer. Cover with the remaining cabbage mixture. Fold the overhanging cabbage leaves over to enclose the "gâteau" completely.

Cover the pan with aluminum foil. Bake for 1 hour. Turn out onto a serving platter. Serve hot, cut in wedges.

SWEET POTATO HASH

Here's a variation on the ever-popular potato hash recipe. Try this for vegetarian Thanksgiving celebrations.

3 lbs. **ORANGE-FLESHED SWEET POTATOES IN THEIR SKINS**
¾ cup **UNSALTED BUTTER**
SALT AND PEPPER

Preheat the oven to 350°. Bake the sweet potatoes in their skins for 45 minutes.

Meanwhile, clarify the butter by melting it in a small saucepan over low heat. Let it cool and settle for about 1 minute. Carefully pour the liquid into a bowl, leaving the unwanted solids in the pan.

When the sweet potatoes are cool enough to handle, peel them. Cut the flesh into 1-inch cubes.

Heat the clarified butter in a large skillet or wok over a medium heat. Stir-fry the sweet potato cubes for 5 to 10 minutes, until crispy and golden.

Season with salt and pepper. Transfer to a warmed serving dish and serve immediately.

CARROTS BRAISED IN OLIVE OIL WITH ROSEMARY AND GARLIC

The long, slow cooking of this easy recipe transforms a simple root vegetable into a very tasty dish, which may also be served hot or cool as a first course.

3 tbl. **EXTRA-VIRGIN OLIVE OIL**
6½ cups **CARROTS CUT INTO SMALL STICKS** (1½ lbs.)
2 **GARLIC CLOVES, CRUSHED**
JUICE AND THIN STRIP OF FINELY PARED PEEL FROM AN UNWAXED LEMON, ABOUT 3 inches LONG
1 tbl. **FINELY CHOPPED FRESH ROSEMARY NEEDLES OR 1½ tsp. DRIED**
SALT AND PEPPER
SPRIG OF ROSEMARY, TO GARNISH (OPTIONAL)

Put all the ingredients, except half the lemon juice, in a heavy-based saucepan covered with a tight-fitting lid.

Cook over the lowest possible heat for 1 hour, stirring occasionally.

Just before serving remove the strip of lemon peel. Stir in the remaining lemon juice. Garnish with a rosemary sprig, if using.

FRESH PEACH PAVLOVA

This gorgeous, gooey confection of meringue and cream, named after the ballerina while she was on a trip "down under," is always a surefire success as a spectacular party dessert. Made with fresh peaches it comes near to perfection.

Use the leftover egg yolks to make the Cappuccino Ice Cream on page 115.

Serves 6 to 10

6 EGG WHITES

1½ cups SUPERFINE SUGAR

PINCH OF SALT

1½ tbl. VINEGAR

1¼ cups HEAVY CREAM, WHIPPED

6 SMALL OR 4 LARGE PEACHES, PEELED, PITTED, AND THINLY SLICED

Preheat the oven to 300°.

Cut 4 circles with a diameter of 9 inches from waxed paper. Place a circle in each of two 9-inch springform cake pans. Wet one side of each of the remaining circles and place them, wet side down, on the first circles. (The water sandwiched between the papers makes it easier to remove the paper when the meringues are baked.)

Beat the egg whites with half the sugar, the salt, and the vinegar until very stiff. Add the rest of the sugar and beat again until stiff and glossy.

Spread the meringue on the paper circles, leaving a border about 1 inch clear of the edge. Bake for 30 minutes, then lower the temperature to 275°. Bake for 30 minutes longer.

Remove the meringues from the pans and let them cool on wire racks. Invert and carefully peel off the paper.

Place one meringue circle on a serving plate and spread with half the cream. Arrange half the peach slices on this. Place the remaining meringue circle on top and spread it with the remaining cream. Arrange the rest of the peach slices in concentric circles over the top (like a French apple tart).

COOK-AHEAD CUISINE

For midweek entertaining, or other occasions when the busy cook has little time before the guests arrive for a meal, here is a menu in which most of the recipes can be prepared the day before and involve the minimum of last-minute cooking.

VERY GARLICKY VEGETABLE SOUP

PASTA-STUFFED PEPPERS
LEAF SALAD

JOAN'S SPICE CAKE WITH SEVEN-MINUTE BROWN SUGAR FROSTING

VERY GARLICKY VEGETABLE SOUP

This chunky rustic vegetable soup is so tasty it will vanish in no time, yet it is simplicity itself to make. Don't chicken out (if you will excuse the meatist expression) and use less garlic—the initial blanching removes any harshness and, thus treated, the garlic gives the most wonderful rich flavor to the soup.

16 GARLIC CLOVES

3 tbl. OLIVE OIL

1 LARGE ONION, CHOPPED

2 LARGE LEEKS, COARSELY CHOPPED (INCLUDING GOOD BITS OF GREEN)

2 LARGE CARROTS, COARSELY CHOPPED

2 LARGE CELERY STICKS, COARSELY CHOPPED

1⅓ cups RUTABAGA, CUT INTO BITE-SIZE CHUNKS

3 cups POTATOES CUT INTO BITE-SIZE CHUNKS

2 quarts VEGETABLE STOCK

2½ cups SHREDDED GREEN CABBAGE (ANY KIND)

1½ cups COARSELY CHOPPED TOMATOES

SALT AND PEPPER

FRUITY EXTRA-VIRGIN OLIVE OIL, TO SERVE (OPTIONAL)

Put the garlic cloves in a small saucepan and cover them with cold water. Bring to a boil. Drain and discard the water. Cover again with cold water, bring to a boil again, and drain and discard water. Repeat the process for a third time. Set aside the blanched garlic.

Heat the oil in a very large saucepan over medium heat. Cook the onion for 5 to 10 minutes, stirring occasionally, until softened and just begining to turn golden. Add the leeks, carrots, celery, rutabaga, potatoes, and blanched garlic and continue to cook for 5 minutes longer, stirring constantly.

Add the stock and bring to a boil. Cover the pan and simmer over very low heat for 15 minutes.

Add the cabbage and tomatoes. Cover once more and continue to simmer for 15 minutes longer. Check that all the vegetables are quite tender. Adjust the seasoning if necessary. (Don't forget the stock will already be quite strongly seasoned.)

Serve in warmed bowls or dishes, accompanied by crusty bread. Don't feel you need to add chopped herbs or swirls of cream as this soup simply doesn't need it—its beauty lies in its fresh simplicity. A drizzle of olive oil, however, would not be gilding the lily.

Very Garlicky Vegetable Soup

PASTA-STUFFED PEPPERS

This is a delicious variation on the classic stuffed-vegetable theme, and proves a more substantial main dish than those with the more usual rice-based stuffings. Any type of pasta will do: shells, twists, macaroni, and so on.

6 LARGE RED OR YELLOW BELL PEPPERS, HALVED LENGTHWISE AND SEEDED

4 tbl. DRAINED AND CHOPPED SUN-DRIED TOMATOES IN OIL, OIL RESERVED FOR GREASING

4 tbl. BUTTER

3 ONIONS, CHOPPED

2 tbl. ALL-PURPOSE FLOUR

2 cups MILK

1 cup GRATED SWISS OR GRUYÈRE CHEESE

1 rounded tsp. DRIED HERBES DE PROVENCE

1 cup COOKED PASTA SHAPES (SEE INTRODUCTION)

SALT AND PEPPER

¾ cup GRATED FRESH PARMESAN CHEESE

Preheat the oven to 350°. With a little of the oil from the sun-dried tomatoes, lightly grease a shallow baking dish or baking pan large enough to hold 12 pepper halves in one layer.

Bring a large pan of salted water to a boil. Blanch the pepper halves in it for 3 minutes. Drain them, refresh in cold water, and drain again. Leave them, cut side down, on paper towels to drain until needed.

Meanwhile, melt the butter in a saucepan. Cook the onions over the lowest possible heat for about 20 minutes, stirring occasionally, until they are very soft and pale golden.

Stir in the flour and turn up the heat to medium. Cook for 1 to 2 minutes, stirring constantly. Stir in the milk and bring to a boil. Turn down the heat and simmer, stirring constantly, for 2 to 3 minutes, or until thick and creamy.

Add the grated Swiss or Gruyère cheese, the dried herbs, and the sun-dried tomatoes. Season to taste.

Continue to cook, stirring, for 2 to 3 minutes, until the cheese melts. Stir the cooked pasta into the sauce.

Pile the pasta mixture into the drained pepper halves.

Arrange the stuffed pepper halves in the prepared dish or pan. Sprinkle with the Parmesan cheese. Bake for 40 to 45 minutes, or until the stuffing is bubbling and golden. Serve 2 pepper halves per person.

LEAF SALAD

With the vogue for exotic mixtures of ingredients in salad first courses, plain salads seem to have gone out of fashion. Yet, nothing is nicer to serve on its own after a main course, French style, than a simple salad of fresh tender leaves dressed with a classic vinaigrette.

Supermarkets sell a wonderful selection of trimmed and washed mixed salad leaves in various varieties, so this could not be simpler to prepare. A few fresh herbs snipped over the leaves just before dressing makes a nice change, or you can add a small crushed clove of garlic to the dressing.

4 tbl. VINAIGRETTE (SEE PAGE 18)
4 oz. PREPARED SALAD LEAVES OF CHOICE

Just before sitting down to the meal, pour the dressing into the bottom of a large bowl. Place the salad servers (or whatever is to be used to serve the salad) in the bowl over the dressing and then add the leaves. The salad servers will keep the dressing away from the leaves (because the leaves might go limp if they sit too long in the dressing) until it is time to eat the salad.

At the last moment, toss the salad and serve.

JOAN'S SPICE CAKE WITH SEVEN-MINUTE BROWN SUGAR FROSTING

Joan Campbell is the Food Editor of Vogue Australia *magazine and is one of the best and most innovative cooks in the world. Luckily she is a good friend and occasionally gives me recipes like this delicious easy and foolproof cake, which—amazingly—does not contain any eggs.*

If served on the day it is made, it has a light, fluffy, and crumbly texture; if left for a day or two, it changes completely and becomes moist and fudgy. I like it both ways.

The frosting has an intriguing soft, marshmallow-like texture.

1 cup RAISINS
¾ cup PACKED BROWN SUGAR
   (LIGHT OR DARK)
1 cup plus 1 tbl. UNSALTED BUTTER
1 tsp. VANILLA EXTRACT
3¾ cups ALL-PURPOSE FLOUR, PLUS MORE
   FOR DUSTING
1 tsp. GROUND GINGER
½ tsp. GROUND CINNAMON
½ tsp. GROUND CLOVES
½ tsp. APPLE PIE SPICE
¼ tsp. SALT
1 tsp. BAKING SODA
VEGETABLE OIL FOR GREASING
For the frosting
1 cup BROWN SUGAR (LIGHT OR DARK)
⅛ tsp. GROUND MACE
PINCH OF SALT
⅛ tsp. CREAM OF TARTAR
1 tsp. VANILLA EXTRACT
WHITE OF 1 JUMBO EGG

Preheat the oven to 375°. Oil and flour a 2½-quart ring-shaped cake pan.

Place the raisins, sugar, and butter in a saucepan with 1½ cups water. Bring to a boil. Turn down the heat and simmer for 5 minutes. Let cool completely. Stir in the vanilla extract.

Sift the flour into a large bowl. Add the spices, salt, and baking soda and stir together. Pour in the liquid ingredients and beat together quickly until blended.

Pour the batter into the prepared pan. Bake for 45 minutes, or until a toothpick inserted into the cake comes out dry. Turn out onto a wire rack and let cool.

Meanwhile, make the frosting. Place all the ingredients in a bowl with 2 tbl. of water. Set the bowl over a pan of boiling water. Using an electric mixer, beat for 3 minutes. Remove the bowl from the pan and beat for 4 minutes longer as the frosting cools.

Cover the cooled cake roughly with the frosting.

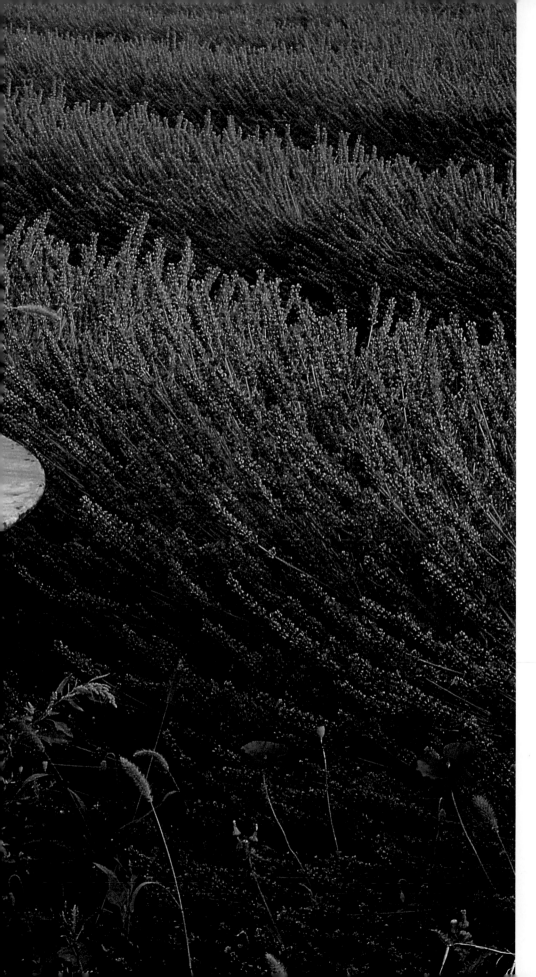

THE FRUITS OF THE FIELDS

This fresh and summery menu celebrates the skills of the market gardener and is a veritable cornucopia of vegetables, herbs, and flowers. Enjoy this meal indoors or out, in winter or summer; whenever or wherever, it conjures up an atmosphere of open fields and countryside, fresh air, and sunshine.

FRESH TOMATO SOUP

ARTICHOKES WITH HOLLANDAISE SAUCE

GARDENER'S LASAGNE

LAVENDER, HONEY, AND GIN ICE CREAM
YUULONG LAVENDER COOKIES

FRESH TOMATO SOUP

One of the nicest and easiest of all soups, this is best made only when really good ripe tasty tomatoes are available. Don't fall into the trap of thinking that if it's "only soup" you are making, second-grade vegetables will do. Certainly it doesn't matter if the tomatoes are a little overripe and squashy, but greenhouse tomatoes without any flavor will only produce a boring, tasteless soup.

If you want to serve this soup for a special occasion, you could remove the skins from the tomatoes, but I never do. If you do not have any basil, use tarragon or parsley.

2 tbl. OLIVE OIL
2 ONIONS, THINLY SLICED
4½ cups CHOPPED REALLY RIPE TOMATOES
   (ABOUT 1½ lbs.)
2¼ quarts VEGETABLE STOCK
SALT AND PEPPER
FRESH BASIL LEAVES, TO GARNISH
   (SEE INTRODUCTION)

Heat the oil in a pan which has a lid. Add the onion, cover the pan, and cook over the lowest possible heat for about 20 minutes, shaking the pan occasionally. The onions must be completely soft, sweet, and dark golden brown.

Add the chopped tomatoes and the stock. Bring to a boil, then reduce the heat and simmer for 3 to 4 minutes. (The tomatoes should not be cooked for too long, to ensure that they retain a fresh taste.) Adjust the seasoning, if necessary.

Serve in warmed bowls, sprinkled with herbs.

ARTICHOKES WITH HOLLANDAISE SAUCE

Artichokes are traditionally served either hot or cold. If served cold, they should be at room temperature, not chilled, and are best accompanied by either a vinaigrette dressing or mayonnaise (with garlic if you like). Hot, they may be served simply with melted butter, with Hollandaise Sauce, or Beurre Blanc (see pages 20 to 21).

Cooking artichokes could not be simpler, but eating them is a little more complicated if you have never tried one before and no one has ever explained the pleasant ritual. This is what you do:

Starting with the outside leaves, pull them off one by one. There is a little bit of soft edible "flesh" at the bottom of each one. Dip this in your chosen sauce, then scrape it off into your mouth with the front teeth. Discard the leaf. (Don't forget to place a large bowl in the middle of the table for the discarded leaves.) Continue until all the leaves have been dealt with. You will now be left with the artichoke bottom, which is the best part. To get at this, however, you must first remove the little brush of chokes which grow from its top. Fingers and a knife are needed here. Discard the choke hairs and then use a knife and fork to enjoy the wonderful meaty base, finishing up the remains of the sauce.

6 GLOBE ARTICHOKES
ABOUT 1¼ cups WARM HOLLANDAISE SAUCE
   (SEE PAGE 20)

Unless you have an enormous pan you will need to fill 2 of your largest pans with salted water; the water will need to come halfway up the artichokes. Bring to a boil.

Cut away the stem of each artichoke as close to the bottom as possible. Arrange the artichokes, bottoms down, in the boiling water. Cover and simmer for 45 minutes.

Remove the cooked artichokes from the pan and drain them upside down for a few minutes. (I stack them in a row on the plate rack over my draining board.)

Serve immediately with the warm Hollandaise Sauce, or leave to cool.

GARDENER'S LASAGNE

This baked pasta dish, with its three layers of different vegetables and rich cheese sauce, is easily as good as the traditional meat-based version—even the most hardened carnivore will be asking for more.

Many people swear by the kind of dried lasagne noodles that do not need any precooking. I find these most unsatisfactory and a very poor substitute for the traditional kind, which, after all, only takes 8 to 9 minutes to cook while you are preparing the rest of the dish.

If you want this recipe to be more substantial, cook 3 extra sheets of lasagne and put them in the bottom of the dish.

9 SHEETS OF TRADITIONAL DRIED LASAGNE
   NOODLES (SEE INTRODUCTION), WEIGHING
   ABOUT 6 oz. IN TOTAL
SALT AND PEPPER
OLIVE OIL FOR GREASING
For the sauce
4 tbl. BUTTER
½ cup ALL-PURPOSE FLOUR
3 cups MILK
1¾ cups GRATED SWISS CHEESE
SCRAPE OF NUTMEG
For filling 1
1 tbl. OLIVE OIL
3 cups SLICED MUSHROOMS
1 tsp. CHOPPED THYME OR
   ½ tsp. DRIED
For filling 2
3 tbl. OLIVE OIL
1 LARGE EGGPLANT, WEIGHING ABOUT 10 oz.,
   CUT ACROSS INTO ½-inch SLICES
For filling 3
1 tbl. OLIVE OIL
1 ONION, CHOPPED
2 GARLIC CLOVES, FINELY CHOPPED
8 oz. FRESH SPINACH

Prehcat the oven to 400°. Oil a baking sheet and a shallow baking dish that measures about 12 × 8 inches.

Cook the noodles in a large pot of boiling salted water, according to the directions on the package, until tender but still very firm. Drain well.

Meanwhile, make the sauce. Melt the butter in a saucepan over medium heat. Stir in the flour. Cook this roux, stirring, for 2 to 3 minutes. Add 2½ cups of the milk and bring to a boil, stirring constantly. (I use a balloon whisk.) When the sauce is thick, turn down the heat to low and simmer, stirring constantly, for 3 to 4 minutes.

Stir in 1 cup of the cheese. Season with salt and pepper and nutmeg. Simmer for 2 to 3 minutes longer, stir-ring, or until the cheese melts and the sauce is smooth. Remove from the heat and stir in the remaining milk.

To make filling 1, heat the oil in a skillet over medium heat. Stir-fry the mushrooms with the thyme for about 5 minutes, or until softened. Season with salt and pepper.

To make filling 2, arrange the egg-plant slices in a layer on the prepared baking sheet and brush them with the oil. Season with salt and pepper. Bake for 15 to 20 minutes, or until softened and lightly browned.

To make filling 3, heat the oil in a wok or large skillet over medium heat. Stir-fry the onion for about 5 minutes, or until soft and translucent. Add the garlic halfway through.

Add the spinach and season with salt and pepper. Turn up the heat and stir-fry for 1 to 2 minutes, or just until the leaves begin to wilt. Do not overcook or the spinach will turn to a mush.

Assemble the lasagne. Spread filling 1 over the bottom of the prepared dish. Pour one-quarter of the sauce over. Cover this with 3 sheets of lasagne noodles. Spread these with filling 2, followed by another quarter of the sauce. Arrange 3 more sheets of noodles over this, then cover with filling 3, followed by one-quarter of the sauce. Top with the remaining 3 sheets of noodles and the remaining sauce.

Sprinkle with the remaining cheese. Bake for about 30 to 40 minutes, or until bubbling and the top is golden.

YUULONG LAVENDER COOKIES

Although I knew that lavender was often included in the popular herbes de Provence *combination, I first became properly acquainted with the idea of flavoring food with lavender on a trip to Australia.*

There I read an article about a lavender farm in Yuulong, near Melbourne, where they make lavender cookies, Fascinated, I wrote to the owners for more details. It turns out that they make between thirteen and fourteen thousand of these cookies each season, and they kindly sent me the recipe.

Makes 30

1 cup BUTTER (WELL WORTH USING BEST- QUALITY UNSALTED)

1 heaping cup of SUPERFINE SUGAR

1 EGG, LIGHTLY BEATEN

1½ cups SELF-RISING FLOUR

1 tbl. DRIED LAVENDER FLOWERS

Preheat the oven to 350°. Line a baking sheet with nonstick parchment paper.

Cream the butter with the sugar. (I do this in my food processor.) Add the egg and beat together. Beat in the flour. Stir in the flowers.

Place small teaspoonfuls of the dough on the prepared baking sheet, allowing space for the cookies to spread. Bake for 15 to 20 minutes, or until the cookies are pale golden in color. Be careful not to let them get too brown; they will not feel crisp to the touch until they cool.

Let the cookies cool on a wire rack. Store in an airtight container (if they ever last that long!).

LAVENDER, HONEY, AND GIN ICE CREAM

This type of ice cream is particularly easy to make, as it doesn't need beating after you put it in the freezer.

Soft enough to serve straight from the freezer, it is delicious on its own but spectacular if served with lavender cookies.

Makes about 1¼ quarts

5 tbl. GIN

1 tbl. DRIED LAVENDER FLOWERS

6 EGG YOLKS

⅔ cup CLEAR HONEY (LAVENDER HONEY IF YOU CAN GET IT, OTHERWISE ANY GOOD- QUALITY FLOWER HONEY WILL DO)

1¼ cups HEAVY CREAM

ANY EDIBLE FLOWERS, TO GARNISH (OPTIONAL)

Warm the gin slightly in a small saucepan, then pour it over the lavender in a small bowl. Cover tightly with plastic wrap and leave to infuse for 1 hour.

Strain the flavored gin through a fine strainer, pressing the lavender flowers against the strainer with the back of the spoon to extract all the flavor; discard the flowers. You should end up with about 3 tbl. of strongly flavored gin. If it is a little under, top it up with a drop or two of plain gin.

In a large bowl, beat the egg yolks until very light and fluffy. (An electric mixer makes it easy, otherwise use a wire balloon whisk.) In a small saucepan, heat the honey until just boiling.

Pour the hot honey in a thin steady stream over the egg yolks, beating constantly. Keep beating vigorously until the mixture cools and the yolks increase in volume; this should take 2 to 3 minutes using an electric mixer, but unfortunately at least 5 to 10 minutes by hand. Add the flavored gin and stir together.

Whip the cream until soft peaks form. Carefully fold it into the egg yolk mixture until blended. Pour the mixture into a freezer proof bowl or other suitable container. Freeze for at least 8 hours.

Garnish with fresh flowers, if using, to serve.

Lavender, Honey, and Gin Ice Cream with Yuulong Lavender Cookies

HARVEST HOME

This menu has more than a hint of autumn, of mists and mellow fruitfulness. Containing a collection of full-blown flavors to satisfy the heartiest of appetites, it is a meal to celebrate a season of harvests safely gathered in—when the evenings are drawing in, sitting in the soft glow of candlelight, perhaps with a log crackling on the fire.

CREAM OF SCORCHED PEPPER SOUP

CHEESE AND ONION "SAUSAGES"
YORKSHIRE PUDDINGS
MASHED POTATOES WITH OLIVES, OLIVE OIL, AND PARMESAN
ONION AND SUN-DRIED TOMATO GRAVY
SEASONAL VEGETABLES

CODDLED PEARS IN SPICED RUM SAUCE

CREAM OF SCORCHED PEPPER SOUP

**4 LARGE RIPE RED OR YELLOW
    BELL PEPPERS**

2 tbl. EXTRA-VIRGIN OLIVE OIL

**4 SHALLOTS OR 1 MEDIUM
    ONION, CHOPPED**

**1 tsp. FRESH THYME LEAVES
    OR ½ tsp. DRIED**

2 GARLIC CLOVES, CRUSHED

5 cups VEGETABLE STOCK

2½ cups MILK

SALT AND PEPPER

**FRESH BASIL LEAVES OR OTHER
    HERBS, TO GARNISH**

Preheat a hot broiler.

Cut the peppers lengthwise in quarters; discard the seeds and white membranes. Arrange the quarters, skin-side up, on the broiler rack. Broil until all the skin is blackened and blistered.

Transfer to a plastic bag, close and leave for 5 minutes. The blackened skins will now come away easily and can be discarded. Do not rinse the peppers or you will wash away the precious juices.

Meanwhile, heat the oil in a large heavy-bottomed saucepan over low heat. Cook the shallots or onion, stirring occasionally, for 5 to 10 minutes, until soft and translucent.

Add the thyme, garlic, stock, and all but one piece of the skinned peppers. Bring to a boil, then simmer for 20 minutes.

Purée the soup in a food processor or blender in batches. Return to the rinsed-out pan. Add the milk and reheat. Season to taste.

Cut the reserved piece of pepper into thin strips.

Pour the soup into 6 warmed bowls. Garnish with the pepper strips and the fresh herbs.

CHEESE AND ONION "SAUSAGES"

These tasty "sausages" do not need to apologize for being a meat substitute, because they are good enough to stand up in their own right. Quick and easy to make, you can serve these as a main course with potatoes and vegetables. Set on a bed of chopped fresh tomatoes, and dressed with a garlicky vinaigrette, they also make a satisfying supper dish.

Makes 6 to 8 sausages

**1 cup GRATED SHARP CHEDDAR CHEESE, OR
    ANY OTHER TASTY HARD CHEESE**

3 cups FRESH WHITE BREAD CRUMBS

**1 SMALL MILD ONION, VERY
    FINELY CHOPPED**

¼ tsp. DRY MUSTARD

1 tbl. CHOPPED PARSLEY

2 EGGS

4 tbl. MILK
SALT AND PEPPER
ALL-PURPOSE FLOUR FOR COATING
OIL FOR FRYING

In a bowl, mix together the cheese, bread crumbs, onion, mustard, and parsley. Season well with salt and pepper.

Mix one whole egg and the yolk of the other (reserve the white) with the milk. Add this to the cheese mixture and stir.

Form the mixture into 6 or 8 thick link sausage shapes. Beat the egg white lightly. Dip the ''sausages'' into it. Next, roll them in flour, shaking off any excess.

Fry the ''sausages'' in hot oil for about 10 minutes, turning them occasionally so they brown on all sides.

Cheese and Onion "Sausages" with Yorkshire Puddings (page 70) and Onion and Sun-Dried Tomato Gravy (page 70) served with seasonal vegetables.

YORKSHIRE PUDDINGS

Why should something so totally delicious be reserved for meat eaters? Yorkshire puddings taste just as good without the roast beef. In fact, they were traditionally served on their own as a first course, to take the edge off appetites before the expensive meat course was brought to the table.

Probably the most traditional way of cooking Yorkshire pudding is in one big rectangular baking sheet, cutting it into squares to serve it, but I prefer to cook mine in muffin pans. This provides a crisper outside and less puddingy middle.

Makes 18 to 20 puddings
1 cup ALL-PURPOSE FLOUR
PINCH OF SALT
2 EGGS
1¼ cups MILK OR ROUGHLY EQUAL
   QUANTITIES MILK AND WATER
2 tbl. VEGETABLE OIL

Sift the flour and salt into a bowl. Add the eggs and half the liquid. Beat well for 2 to 3 minutes.

Gradually add the remaining liquid and beat together. (All this can be done in seconds in a food processor.) Leave the batter to rest for about 1 hour.

Preheat the oven to 425°.

Pour a few drops of oil into each section of 2 trays of muffin cups. (If making one big pudding, use all the oil in a roasting pan measuring about 11 × 7 inches.) Place them in the preheated oven and leave at least 5 minutes until very hot.

Beat the batter again briefly. Remove the muffin trays from the oven and, working as quickly as possible, put about 1 tbl. of batter into as many muffin cups as possible; add 1 tbl. water to any unfilled cups. Return to the oven for 15 to 20 minutes (30 to 40 minutes for a big one), until well risen and nice and brown.

Serve immediately.

MASHED POTATOES WITH OLIVES, OLIVE OIL, AND PARMESAN

It isn't necessary to go all the way to Italy to eat good Italian food. Stephano Cavallini, a talented chef in London, kindly gave me this recipe, which transforms a very ordinary dish like mashed potatoes into a totally Mediterranean treat.

These mashed potatoes are very rich and this recipe produces quite small helpings—double the quantities for hearty eaters!

1½ lbs. POTATOES
2 tbl. EXTRA-VIRGIN OLIVE OIL
1 tbl. LIGHT OR WHIPPING CREAM
¼ cup PITTED GREEN OLIVES CUT INTO
   TINY STRIPS
¼ cup PITTED RIPE OLIVES CUT INTO
   TINY STRIPS
¼ cup FRESHLY GRATED PARMESAN CHEESE
SALT AND PEPPER

Wash the potatoes well, but leave their skins on.

Cook the potatoes in boiling salted water until tender. Drain and peel. Press the hot potatoes through a fine metal strainer with the back of a spoon.

Stir in the oil, cream, olives, and Parmesan. Season to taste with salt and pepper. (Remember that Parmesan is quite salty, so go steady with the salt.)

ONION AND SUN-DRIED TOMATO GRAVY

What would Yorkshire puddings be without lots of good hot gravy? This gravy is as hearty and flavorsome as any made from meat drippings, and makes an excellent sauce to pour over all sorts of food.

1 tbl. EXTRA-VIRGIN OLIVE OIL
1 LARGE ONION, CHOPPED
⅓ cup DRAINED AND CHOPPED SUN-DRIED
   TOMATOES IN OIL
2½ cups VEGETABLE STOCK
3 tbl. LIGHT CREAM
SALT AND PEPPER

Heat the oil in a heavy-bottomed pan which has a lid over medium heat. Cook the onion, stirring constantly, for 5 to 10 minutes, or until brown but not burned.

Add the sun-dried tomatoes and stock. Bring to a boil, then cover and simmer for 15 minutes.

Purée the contents of the pan in a food processor or blender. Return the purée to the pan. Season to taste and stir in the cream.

Reheat the gravy and pour into a gravy boat or serving pitcher.

CODDLED PEARS IN SPICED RUM SAUCE

These poached pears are very easy to prepare, but it is best if you start them the day before you plan to serve them. For a special occasion, decorate the stem of each pear with a bow of thin ribbon, or garnish them with mint or lemon balm leaves, or edible flowers.

¾ cup plus 2 tbl. SUGAR

¼ tsp. SALT

PIECE OF CINNAMON STICK,
   ABOUT 4 inches LONG

4 WHOLE CLOVES

¼ tsp. ALLSPICE BERRIES

PIECE OF GINGER ROOT, ABOUT ½ inch
   ACROSS, PEELED AND SLICED

6 FIRM PEARS, PEELED BUT WITH
   STEMS LEFT ON

7 tbl. RUM

ICE CREAM, YOGURT, FROMAGE
   FRAIS, OR WHIPPED CREAM, TO
   SERVE (OPTIONAL)

Into a large saucepan which has a lid, put the sugar, salt, spices, and 2½ quarts water. Bring to a boil. Cover, turn down the heat, and simmer for 15 minutes.

Put the pears in the saucepan, standing them upright in the syrup. Cook, covered, over low to medium heat, until the pears are quite tender. The exact cooking time will vary very much, according to the type and firmness of the pears, but will probably be 30 minutes to 1 hour. Do not worry if the pointed ends of the pears stick out above the syrup, because they do not need as much cooking as the bottoms and will cook in the steam.

Remove the pears from the syrup and stand them on a plate. Strain the syrup into a clean pan large enough to hold the pears snugly in one layer. Discard the spices and stir the rum into the syrup.

Return the pears to the syrup and leave until quite cool (preferably 4 to 8 hours for the flavors to develop fully). Transfer the pears to a plate and chill.

Place the saucepan of syrup over high heat and boil rapidly to reduce the syrup to 1¼ cups. Let cool and chill.

To serve, place each pear upright on a plate or in a shallow dish. Pour the syrup over and add ice cream, yogurt, or so on, if liked. Garnish as described in the introduction.

Coddled Pears in Spiced Rum Sauce

THROUGH THE LOOKING GLASS

Not all is what it seems at first sight in this topsy-turvy menu: what was once an upside-down apple tart has been turned on its head once more to become a spectacular savory first course; schnitzels exchange meat for layers of vegetables and cheese; and in this Alice-in-Wonderland meal, even a simple fruit pudding has turned to drink!

"TARTE TATIN" OF CARAMELIZED PINK ONIONS AND SUN-DRIED TOMATOES

"SCHNITZELS" OF GRUYÈRE-STUFFED EGGPLANT
MANGO AND CUCUMBER SALSA
GOLDEN RAISIN AND PINE NUT PILAF WITH ROSEMARY

MELON IN GINGER WINE WITH PRESERVED GINGER

"TARTE TATIN" OF CARAMELIZED PINK ONIONS AND SUN-DRIED TOMATOES

The classic Tarte Tatin is an upside-down tart made from caramelized apples and puff pastry. This is my savory version which tastes just as good as it looks. If you can't get pink onions, leeks work equally well.

2 tbl. BUTTER

6 cups EVEN-SIZED PINK ONIONS CUT INTO
   ¾-inch SLICES (ABOUT 2 lbs.)

2 tbl. SUGAR

⅓ cup DRAINED AND COARSELY CHOPPED
   SUN-DRIED TOMATOES IN OIL

8 oz. FROZEN PUFF PASTRY DOUGH,
   DEFROSTED

OLIVE OIL FOR GREASING

SALAD LEAVES, TO GARNISH

Melt the butter in a skillet or sauté pan large enough to accommodate the onion slices snugly in one layer; if you do not have a big enough pan, work in 2 batches.

Sprinkle half the sugar over the onions. Season them with salt and pepper, then pour in enough cold water barely to cover the onions.

Bring to a boil. Reduce the heat and simmer, undisturbed, for about 30 minutes, or until the onions are tender and all the liquid has evaporated to leave a sticky glaze. Keep a careful eye on the pan toward the end of cooking time because the onions can easily burn.

Liberally oil the bottom of a large tart pan or other suitable ovenproof dish. (I use a paella pan with a 9-inch diameter base.) Sprinkle the bottom evenly with the remaining sugar. Sprinkle with the pieces of sun-dried tomato.

Carefully arrange the onion slices on top in the prepared pan. Season with salt and pepper.

Roll out the pastry thinly. Cut out a circle just a little larger than the size of the pan. Arrange this over the onions, tucking in the edges. Chill until required.

Preheat the oven to 425°.

Bake for 20 to 30 minutes, or until the pastry is crisp and golden.

Turn out onto a warmed serving plate. Serve hot, cut in wedges, with a few salad leaves as garnish.

"SCHNITZELS" OF GRUYÈRE-STUFFED EGGPLANT

I love eggplant in all its guises. Like the mushroom, it has a succulent texture which can easily replace meat in a vegetarian menu. These "meaty" sandwiches of vegetable and cheese combine a crispy golden exterior with a melting, gooey center—almost a vegetarian chicken Kiev.

4 MEDIUM EGGPLANTS (ABOUT 2 lbs. IN TOTAL)

1 cup GRATED GRUYÈRE OR SWISS CHEESE

2 EGGS, BEATEN

3 cups FINE WHITE BREAD CRUMBS

SALT AND PEPPER

ALL-PURPOSE FLOUR FOR COATING

EXTRA-VIRGIN OLIVE OIL FOR FRYING AND
   GREASING

Cut each eggplant across diagonally into 6 slices about ¾-inch thick. Sprinkle them with salt and leave for 1 hour in a colander over the sink; the salt draws out some of the bitter juices. Rinse well and pat dry with dish towels.

Preheat the oven to 400°. Grease 2 baking sheets with oil.

Arrange 12 eggplant slices on the counter. Divide the cheese between them, then place the remaining 12 egg-plant slices on top to make "sandwiches."

Season some flour in a shallow bowl. Put the eggs and the bread crumbs into separate bowls. Dip the sandwiches first in the seasoned flour, then in the egg and then in the crumbs, shaking off the excess each time.

Heat a little olive oil in a large skillet. Working in manageable batches and adding a little more oil when necessary, fry the "sandwiches" for 2 minutes on each side. Transfer them to the greased baking sheets. Bake for 20 minutes.

Serve immediately, with the salsa.

MANGO AND CUCUMBER SALSA

A salsa is really just an uncooked sauce or relish, but they seem to be appearing more and more on the menus of popular, fashionable restaurants. This one is really quick to make and incredibly versatile. It is particularly good with crisp fried foods.

½ CUCUMBER

1 LARGE RIPE MANGO, PEELED,
   PITTED AND FINELY CHOPPED

1 SMALL MILD ONION, THINLY
   SLICED AND SEPARATED INTO
   RINGS

2 MEDIUM FRESH CHILI PEPPERS
   (OR MORE TO TASTE), SEEDED
   AND FINELY CHOPPED

JUICE OF 1 LIME OR LEMON

SALT

Using a swivel-bladed vegetable peeler, cut the cucumber into long, thin strips.

Put these strips in a colander. Sprinkle them liberally with salt and leave to drain for 30 minutes; this draws out the water and makes them wilt.

Rinse well under cold running water, drain again, and pat dry with a dish towel.

Transfer the cucumber strips to a bowl. Add all the remaining ingredients and stir together. Cover and chill for at least 2 hours, or preferably overnight, to let the flavors develop.

GOLDEN RAISIN AND PINE NUT PILAF WITH ROSEMARY

Many years ago I ate the most sublime pilaf in a small waterfront restaurant on the south coast of Turkey. It was studded with pine nuts—the first I had encountered—and seemed strongly perfumed with a pine-like flavor.

It was not until years later that I realized that the mysterious flavor came not from the pine nuts but from rosemary. This is my version of that dish.

2 tbl. EXTRA-VIRGIN OLIVE OIL
1 LARGE ONION, CHOPPED
2 cups BASMATI RICE, RINSED AND DRIED
½ cup GOLDEN RAISINS
¾ cup PINE NUTS
1 rounded tsp. FINELY CHOPPED
   FRESH ROSEMARY NEEDLES OR ¾ tsp. DRIED
5 cups VEGETABLE STOCK
1 rounded tbl. CHOPPED PARSLEY
SALT AND PEPPER

Heat the oil in a large heavy-bottomed saucepan which has a lid over medium heat. Cook the onion, stirring occasionally, for about 5 minutes, or until soft and translucent.

Add the rice and continue to cook, stirring, for 3 to 4 minutes longer, or until each grain is coated with oil. Add the golden raisins, pine nuts, rosemary, and stock. Stir together.

Bring to a boil and cook, uncovered and undisturbed, over high heat for about 10 minutes.

When all the stock has boiled away and the surface of the rice is pitted with little holes, turn off the heat and place a dish towel or 2 layers of paper towels over the top of the pan. Cover with the lid and leave for 30 minutes, during which time the rice will continue to cook in its own steam.

Fluff up the rice with a fork. It will now be perfectly cooked. Season if necessary; the stock may have seasoned the rice sufficiently.

Spoon the pilaf into a warmed serving dish. Sprinkle with the parsley and serve.

MELON IN GINGER WINE WITH PRESERVED GINGER

It is an English tradition to serve a wedge of melon dusted with ground ginger as a first course at a formal dinner or lunch. Here, this luscious fruit appears at the other end of the menu, again partnered by ginger—this time in a rather more exotic guise.

For an even prettier effect, mix melons with differently colored flesh, such as cantaloupe with watermelon.

Ginger wine is a grape wine that has been flavored with fruits, herbs, and spices. It isn't widely available and you will probably have to contact specialty wine merchants who sell European imports. The search, however, will be worth the effort for a special occasion.

If you can't find ginger wine, however, do not substitute ginger ale. Instead, stir together some of the syrup from the jar with a little dry sherry or dry vermouth.

1 LARGE OR 2 SMALL MELONS,
   HALVED, PEELED, AND SEEDED
12 PIECES OF PRESERVED GINGER IN
   SYRUP, DRAINED AND CHOPPED
1 cup GINGER WINE (SEE INTRODUCTION)

Cut the melon flesh into bite-size cubes. Put the melon cubes in an attractive serving dish (glass looks lovely) or divide them between 6 wine glasses. Sprinkle with the chopped preserved ginger. Pour the ginger wine over.

Chill for at least 2 hours, or up to 12, before serving.

RIGHT: *Melon in Ginger Wine with Preserved Ginger*

THE BREADWINNER

Sometimes a little lateral thinking is called for when it comes to dreaming up new ideas for vegetarian main courses. Here a classic, old-fashioned dessert takes on a new role, swapping sugar and spice for all things nice in a savory way to become a mouthwatering garlic-perfumed centerpiece to this three-course menu.

RADISHES AND CORN WAFERS WITH THREE PÂTÉS

SAVORY BREAD-AND-BUTTER PUDDING
SEASONAL VEGETABLES

FRESH FIGS WITH RUM AND MASCARPONE

RADISHES AND CORN WAFERS WITH THREE PÂTÉS

These crisp and golden cracker-like wafers take only seconds to make. They are traditionally made with cornmeal, but this can vary in quality and in the amount of water it will absorb. For this reason I make mine with "easy-cook" polenta, available from Italian food stores and delicatessens and pretty much the same thing.

I like to serve these with a variety of pâtés, such as the three recipes given in the Breads and Basics chapter (see pages 22 to 24), but just one will do. Alternatively, offer a selection of dips.

Makes about 12 wafers

2 tbl. BUTTER, MELTED, PLUS
   MORE FOR GREASING
1 cup "EASY-COOK" POLENTA
   (SEE INTRODUCTION)
½ tsp. SALT
¼ tsp. CHILI POWDER
1½ cups BOILING WATER
2 BUNCHES OF PINK RADISHES,
   TO SERVE
PÂTÉS OR DIPS, TO SERVE (SEE
   INTRODUCTION)

Preheat the oven to 400°. Grease 2 or 3 baking sheets with butter.

Put the polenta in a heatproof bowl with the salt and chili powder. Pour the boiling water over and stir vigorously to avoid lumps forming. Stir in the butter. The batter should be the consistency of light cream; if it is too thick, stir in a little more cold water.

Pour tablespoonfuls of the batter onto the prepared baking sheets and spread each out as thinly as possible to make circles. You will probably only get 4 or 5 easily on each baking sheet, so bake them in batches.

Bake for about 20 minutes, or until the edges just begin to turn brown and crispy. Transfer to a wire rack to let them cool; they will become crisp as they cool.

Serve with the radishes and pâtés or dips.

SAVORY BREAD-AND-BUTTER PUDDING

A clever twist on an old favorite, this unusual main course is inexpensive, tasty, and satisfying. Cooked endive gives a particularly savory and distinctive flavor to the creamy custard.

4 tbl. BUTTER, PLUS MORE FOR GREASING
1 cup FINELY DICED CARROT
1¼ cups SLICED LEEK (ABOUT 1 LARGE LEEK)
1¼ cups SLICED BELGIAN ENDIVE
   (ABOUT 2 SMALL HEADS)
JUICE OF ½ LEMON
1 tbl. SUGAR
4 oz. ITALIAN CIABATTA OR FRENCH BREAD,
   CUT INTO SLICES ABOUT ¼ inch THICK

3 EGGS, LIGHTLY BEATEN
1¼ cups MILK
1¼ cups LIGHT CREAM
2 GARLIC CLOVES, CRUSHED
SALT AND PEPPER

Preheat the oven to 325°. Grease a deep baking dish with butter.

Melt half the butter over a medium heat in a heavy-bottomed saucepan which has a lid. Stir-fry the carrot for 2 minutes.

Add the leek, endive, lemon juice, and sugar. Season well with salt and pepper. Turn down the heat as low as possible, cover the pan, and gently cook the vegetables, stirring occasionally, for 10 to 15 minutes, or until quite soft.

Spread the remaining butter on the slices of bread.

Arrange half the bread slices, buttered side up, in the bottom of the prepared dish. Arrange the cooked vegetables on top of the bread. Cover with the remaining slices of bread, buttered side up.

Beat the eggs with the milk, cream, and garlic. Season with salt and pepper. Pour this over the contents of the dish. Bake for 1¼ to 1½ hours, or until the custard is set and the top is crisp and golden.

LEFT: *Savory Bread-and-Butter Pudding;* RIGHT: *Fresh Figs with Rum and Mascarpone (page 85)*

FRESH FIGS WITH RUM AND MASCARPONE

I discovered this recipe in a tiny restaurant in the mountains of Liguria in northwest Italy, where I ate a splendid lunch outside one perfect day in late summer and the figs were still warm from the tree. Try this whenever you see fresh figs on sale—even better if you can pick them yourself when vacationing in a fig-producing area!

24 VERY RIPE, LARGE FIGS
  (PREFERABLY BLACK)
6 tbl. (OR MORE) DARK RUM
6 tbl. (OR MORE) MASCARPONE
  CHEESE

Cut a deep cross in the top of each fig. Put 4 figs in each of 6 bowls.

Drizzle the rum over. Spoon the mascarpone onto the plate and serve.

FARMER'S BASKET

Imagine a small country market in a Mediterranean village . . . think of stalls groaning with fat ripe fruit and vegetables, sun-ripened, tight-skinned, and bursting with goodness . . . and you have the first course of this menu.

A basket of the freshest of free-range eggs becomes the second course, and for the dessert we raid the orchards and meadows of northern France for apples, Calvados, and rich, fresh cream.

CAPONATA

GRATIN OF EGGS WITH SMOTHERED ONIONS AND ROQUEFORT BASMATI RICE

APPLE TARTS WITH CALVADOS CREAM SAUCE

CAPONATA

I adore all kinds of Italian food, particularly the thousands of inventive and delicious ways in which they prepare and cook vegetables. A good example is this wonderful sweet-and-sour dish from the spectacularly beautiful island of Sicily. The only traditional ingredient which must be left out to make this a vegetarian dish is the anchovy, but there are so many other flavorsome ingredients that the loss is barely noticeable.

3½ cups EGGPLANT CUT INTO 1-inch CUBES
4 tbl. EXTRA-VIRGIN OLIVE OIL
4 CELERY STALKS, CUT INTO ½-inch PIECES
1 LARGE ONION, CHOPPED
3 tbl. SUGAR
5 tbl. RED-WINE VINEGAR
14-ounce CAN ITALIAN PEELED TOMATOES, DRAINED
2 tbl. TOMATO PASTE
1 cup LARGE PITTED GREEN OLIVES
2 tbl. GOLDEN RAISINS
1½ tbl. CAPERS
½ cup PINE NUTS
SALT AND PEPPER
CHOPPED FLAT-LEAF PARSLEY, TO GARNISH
LEMON WEDGES, TO SERVE

Place the eggplant cubes in a colander. Sprinkle them generously with salt and leave for 1 hour to draw out any bitter juices. Rinse well and pat dry.

Caponata

cooked vegetables to the pan.

Combine the sugar and vinegar. Add this to the pan together with the tomatoes, tomato paste, olives, golden raisins, and capers. Season well with salt and pepper. Bring to a boil. Reduce the heat and simmer, stirring frequently, for 15 minutes. Stir in the pine nuts.

Transfer to a serving dish and let cool. Garnish with parsley and lemon wedges to serve.

GRATIN OF EGGS WITH SMOTHERED ONIONS AND ROQUEFORT

The success of this simple dish lies in the long, slow cooking of the onions, because this renders them sweet and melting to contrast superbly with the strong, sharp flavor of the cheese in the sauce.

You can make this in one large gratin dish, or 6 individual ones for a more formal presentation. For a special occasion, replace the more usual hen eggs with quail eggs, available from some delicatessens and gourmet food stores.

3 tbl. **EXTRA-VIRGIN OLIVE OIL**

6 cups **SLICED ONIONS**

7 tbl. **BUTTER, PLUS MORE FOR GREASING**

9 **LARGE HARD-BOILED EGGS,**
  SHELLED AND HALVED, OR 36
  WHOLE HARD-BOILED QUAIL
  EGGS (SEE INTRODUCTION), SHELLED

½ cup **ALL-PURPOSE FLOUR**

2½ cups **MILK**

1 cup **CRUMBLED ROQUEFORT CHEESE**

1 cup **FRESH BREAD CRUMBS,**
  PREFERABLY WHITE

SALT AND PEPPER

Heat half the oil in a large skillet or wok over medium heat. Stir-fry the celery for 10 minutes. Add the onion and continue to cook, stirring frequently, for 10 minutes longer, or until the onion is soft and golden.

Remove the cooked vegetables from the pan with a slotted spoon and transfer them to a bowl.

Heat the remaining oil in the pan. Cook the dried eggplant cubes over medium heat, stirring frequently, for 8 to 10 minutes, or until golden. Return the

Heat the oil over medium heat in a large, heavy-bottomed saucepan which has a lid. Add the onions. Season with salt and pepper and cook, stirring, for 5 to 10 minutes, or until the onions just begin to soften.

Turn down the heat as low as possible and press a circle of waxed paper or a butter parchment paper down on top of the onions. Put the lid on the pan and leave the onions to cook for about 1 hour, removing the paper and stirring the onions occasionally. (The paper holds in the steam, which helps the onions to cook without burning.) The cooked onions should be very soft and a rich golden brown.

Toward the end of the onion cooking time, preheat the oven to 350°. Grease one large baking dish or 6 individual ones with butter.

Smooth the cooked onions over the bottom of the prepared dish(es). Arrange the eggs on top of the onions.

Melt two-thirds of the butter in a clean saucepan. Add the flour and cook this roux over medium heat for 2 to 3 minutes, stirring constantly. Add the milk and bring to a boil, stirring constantly. (I use a balloon whisk for this job.) When the sauce is thick, turn down the heat and simmer it for about 5 minutes. Stir in the cheese. Season the sauce with salt and pepper. Continue to cook, stirring, for 2 to 3 minutes longer, or just until the cheese melts and the sauce is smooth.

Pour the sauce over the eggs. Sprinkle with the bread crumbs and dot with the remaining butter, cut into small pieces.

Bake for about 30 minutes, or until crisp, golden, and bubbling. Serve with plain boiled or steamed Basmati rice.

APPLE TARTS WITH CALVADOS CREAM SAUCE

This wonderful variation on a classic recipe from Normandy was given to me by chef Jean-Pierre Lelettier of the Hôtel de France at des Fuchsias.

Of course, Jean-Pierre made his own puff pastry—and you can if you are good at it—but it is much simpler to buy the frozen variety available in supermarkets, which comes already rolled out in separate sheets.

Calvados, the apple brandy from Normandy, is available from liquor stores.

**6 SHEETS OF DEFROSTED PUFF PASTRY
DOUGH (SEE INTRODUCTION)**

6 DESSERT APPLES

4 tbl. STRAINED APRICOT JAM

For the sauce

7 tbl. SUGAR

1¼ cups LIGHT CREAM

2 tbl. CALVADOS OR BRANDY

For the purée

**3 DESSERT APPLES, PEELED, CORED,
AND CHOPPED**

2 tbl. BUTTER

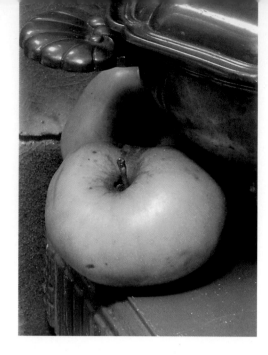

First make the sauce. Put the sugar in a small pan with just enough water to dissolve it. Cook over medium heat, without stirring, until a golden caramel is formed.

Pour in all the cream at once; the caramel will solidify. Bring to a boil. Then turn down the heat and simmer, stirring constantly, for 2 to 3 minutes, until the caramel dissolves. Remove the pan from the heat and add the Calvados or brandy. Let cool. Cover and chill.

Preheat the oven to 400°.

Using a 6-inch saucer or paper template as a guide, cut out 6 circles from the rolled-out pastry dough; take care not to drag the knife. Arrange these on a dampened baking sheet and chill until required.

Make the purée. Peel, core, and chop the apples. Cook the apple slices 2 tbl. of water and the butter over very low heat for 10 to 15 minutes, or until mushy. Purée in a food processor or blender, or mash with a potato masher. Let cool.

Place the apple halves, cut side down, on a chopping board in front of you; the cavity should be turned away from you. Starting on the right-hand side (left if you are left-handed), using a knife blade pointing away from you, slice the apple as thinly as possible, gradually angling the tip of the knife to the left (or right, if left-handed) as you slice. The cuts should end up in a slight fan shape. Push the sliced apple half over like a pack of cards and it will fan out to make a perfect semicircle.

Put 1 tbl. of the purée on each dough circle, spreading it evenly but leaving a clear 1-inch border all the way around. Arrange 2 semicircles of apple slices over the purée; these should cover the purée almost completely and make a circle.

Bake for about 20 minutes, or until the apple is tender and the pastry border is golden brown.

Toward the end of this time, melt the jam in a small pan with 2 tbl. of water. As soon as the tarts come out of the oven, brush them all over with the jam to glaze.

To serve, pour the chilled sauce onto 6 large plates. Place a warm tart on top and serve immediately.

Apple Tart with Calvados Cream Sauce

THE COLORS OF SUMMER

Food should not only smell and taste appetizing, but look good, too! Nothing could look more gorgeous than this colorful procession of delicious dishes —crimson tomatoes, golden polenta, a brilliant salad of primary colors, and the jewel-like hues of glistening summer fruits—in a menu to delight both the eye and the palate.

TOMATO AND BASIL SALAD

Few flavor combinations can be more perfect than that of tomatoes and basil. And what could be better—or easier—to start a summer meal than this classic salad.

It does, however, rely on superb ripe tomatoes. If you can only find greenhouse tomatoes, don't bother.

The sun-dried tomatoes in this recipe are far from classic, but they give the salad a bit of "bite" and emphasize the tomato flavor.

2 lbs. RIPE TOMATOES (SEE INTRODUCTION), SLICED

4 tbl. VINAIGRETTE (SEE PAGE 18)

1 GARLIC CLOVE, CRUSHED

2 tbl. DRAINED AND CHOPPED SUN-DRIED TOMATOES IN OIL (OPTIONAL—SEE INTRODUCTION)

2 tbl. (OR MORE) FRESH BASIL LEAVES

Arrange the tomato slices on an serving plate or in a shallow dish.

Mix the garlic into the vinaigrette. Drizzle the tomatoes with the dressing. Sprinkle with the sun-dried tomatoes, if using.

Leave for 30 minutes to 1 hour at room temperature to let the flavors develop fully.

Sprinkle with the basil just before serving.

ROSEMARY FOCACCIA

This flat Italian bread is really a very simple pizza. There are almost as many variations on the recipe as there are cooks in Italy. My simple version uses quick-rising active dry yeast, which is added to the dry ingredients and is much easier and quicker to use than the traditional active dry yeast (see page 15).

6 cups WHITE BREAD FLOUR

1 envelope (1 tbl.) QUICK-RISING ACTIVE DRY
    YEAST

1½ tsp. SALT

2 tbl. FRESH ROSEMARY NEEDLES OR 1½ tbl.
    DRIED

3 tbl. EXTRA-VIRGIN OLIVE OIL,
    PLUS MORE FOR GREASING

2 cups VERY WARM WATER (120° to 130°)

KOSHER SEA SALT

Place the flour in a large bowl with the yeast, salt, and half the rosemary. Stir in 2 tbl. of the oil and the water. Bring the dough together to form a ball.

Knead the dough for a good 10 minutes as described on page 15.

Form the dough into a ball and place it on a floured board. Sprinkle with flour and cover with floured plastic wrap or a floured lightweight cloth. Leave it in a warm place (not too warm—just an average kitchen will do) to rise, until about doubled in size (see page 15).

Preheat the oven to 450°. Lightly grease a 15- × 10¾-inch baking sheet with a little oil.

Roll out the dough into a circle on the prepared baking sheet. Leave the dough to rise again for about 1 hour, until doubled in thickness.

With your fingertips, make indentations all over the surface of the dough. Drizzle with the remaining olive oil or paint it on with a brush. Sprinkle with the remaining rosemary and a liberal amount of salt.

Bake for about 15 minutes, or until golden and baked through. Cut into wedges and serve warm or at room temperature.

BROILED POLENTA WITH MUSHROOMS, ARTICHOKES, AND BRIE

Polenta is a type of porridge made from a coarse cornmeal, and is much loved by the Italians who eat it in all kinds of different ways. In this recipe it is left to go cold and set into a loaf, then sliced and broiled until crispy. You can also fry it.

Originally polenta had to be stirred constantly on the top of a stove for a very long time, but now "easy-cook" polenta needs only a fraction of the cooking time. It is available from good Italian delicatessens.

1½ quarts VEGETABLE STOCK

1 tsp. SALT

3¼ cups "EASY-COOK" POLENTA
    (SEE INTRODUCTION)

5 tbl. EXTRA-VIRGIN OLIVE OIL,
    PLUS MORE FOR GREASING

5 cups SLICED MUSHROOMS

2 GARLIC CLOVES, CRUSHED

2 tbl. CHOPPED PARSLEY

8 oz. CANNED ARTICHOKE
    BOTTOMS, DRAINED AND
    THINLY SLICED

1 lb. BRIE, CUT VERTICALLY
    INTO THIN SLICES (INCLUDING
    THE RIND)

SALT AND PEPPER

Put the stock and salt in a heavy-bottomed saucepan over high heat. Bring it to a boil. Stir in the polenta in a slow, steady stream, stirring constantly to prevent lumps forming. Simmer, stirring, for 5 to 10 minutes.

Pour into a greased 8- × 4- × 2½-inch bread pan. Leave for at least 1 hour to cool and set.

Preheat a hot broiler if broiling the polenta.

Turn out the polenta onto a chopping board. Cut off 12 slices about ½ inch thick (save the rest for another day).

Using about 3 tbl. of olive oil in total, brush the polenta slices on both sides. Working in manageable batches, broil the polenta slices for 3 to 4 minutes on each side, until golden and crispy; keep these warm while you cook the rest. (Sometimes I also use a heavy, ridged cast-iron skillet to fry the slices, which produces attractive "grilled" stripes.)

Meanwhile, heat the remaining oil in a skillet or wok over medium heat. Stir-fry the mushrooms, garlic, and parsley for 5 to 10 minutes, until soft. Stir in the artichoke slices. Season with salt and pepper and cook for 1 minute longer.

Preheat the oven to 375°. Grease a baking sheet with oil.

Arrange 6 polenta slices on the prepared baking sheet. Divide the mushroom mixture between them, piling it high and trying to keep it within the confines of the slices. Top with the remaining polenta slices so you make 6 "sandwiches." Place the cheese slices on top of these. Bake for about 5 minutes, or until the cheese melts. Serve immediately with the salad.

GREEN AND ORANGE SALAD

Carrots are not often used in mixed salads. However, grated and combined with lettuce leaves, they add a sweet crunchiness and a fabulous splash of color to the meal table.

If it is the nasturtium season (many supermarkets now sell edible flowers in the produce section, or look for them at an herb garden), buy some because they add extra color and an interesting slightly bitter tang.

**4 oz. GREEN SALAD LEAVES, RINSED, DRIED
   AND TORN INTO SMALLISH PIECES
2 SMALL OR 1 LARGE CARROT, GRATED
4 tbl. VINAIGRETTE (SEE PAGE 18)
NASTURTIUM FLOWERS, TO
   GARNISH (OPTIONAL)**

Toss the leaves and grated carrot together in a salad bowl.

Just before serving, toss the salad ingredients with the vinaigrette dressing. Sprinkle with the nasturtiums, if using.

SUMMER FRUIT SALAD IN PINEAU DES CHARENTES

Pineau des Charentes is a delicious French aperitif wine made in Cognac from a combination of grape juice and brandy. The white version is fruity and grape-like and best served chilled or with ice as an aperitif. The rosé version, which is deep red and rather port-like, is best served at the end of a meal, and is particularly good with cheese.

Not only is pineau good to drink, it is also excellent to use in recipes, both sweet and savory (see also the Passion Fruit and Pineau Syllabub on page 101). Look for it in specialty liquor stores and wine merchants. If you can't find any, substitute dry vermouth with a little honey dissolved in it.

1 ½ to 2 lbs. SUMMER FRUIT, CUT INTO
   BITE-SIZE PIECES
1 ¼ cups WHITE *PINEAU DES CHARENTES*
   (SEE INTRODUCTION)
SUGAR FOR FROSTING

Put the fruit in a bowl with the *pineau des Charentes*. Mix together. Cover with plastic wrap and chill for 3 to 6 hours to let the flavors develop.

Frost the rims of 6 large wine glasses by dipping them first in water and then in sugar.

Divide the fruit between the decorated glasses, making sure everyone gets a good share of ''juice.'' Serve immediately.

PIZZA PARTY

This is a wonderful menu for the sort of informal occasion when family and friends gather with a drink around the barbecue or gossip in the kitchen. They can then help with the pizza topping. This makes a perfect summer party for the young, old, and the rest of us.

BARBECUED VEGETABLE PLATTER

PIZZA OF RADICCHIO, CHÈVRE, TOMATOES, OLIVES, AND CAPERS

PASSION FRUIT AND PINEAU SYLLABUB WITH BURNED-SUGAR SHARDS

BARBECUED VEGETABLE PLATTER

Barbecues are usually associated with meat, but why should vegetarians miss out on the fun? Lots of vegetables are delicious grilled over glowing charcoal!

The list of vegetables here is just intended as a guideline: try your own combinations and add or substitute peppers and eggplants (prepared as on pages 24 and 124 respectively), or whole tomatoes and zucchini sliced on an angle.

In bad weather, or if you don't own a barbecue grill, simply use the broiler in the kitchen.

2 SMALL FENNEL BULBS, HARD
  CORES REMOVED
3 SMALL BELGIAN ENDIVE HEADS
2 SMALL TIGHT HEADS OF
  RADICCHIO, TRIMMED OF ANY
  BRUISED, LOOSE OUTSIDE LEAVES
2/3 cup EXTRA-VIRGIN OLIVE OIL
SALT AND PEPPER
LEMON WEDGES, TO SERVE
SPRIGS OF FRESH HERBS,
  TO GARNISH

Cut the fennel bulbs from top to bottom into 6 slices about ½ inch thick. Cut each head of Belgian endive lengthwise into 4 long wedges, removing most of the hard core, but leaving enough to hold the leaves together. Cut the radicchio heads from top to bottom into 6 slices about ½ inch thick. Any leftover bits of the vegetables can be kept to use in a salad.

Brush the vegetable slices all over with olive oil. Sprinkle with salt and pepper and leave on a plate to marinate for about 30 minutes.

Light the barbecue coals or preheat the broiler.

Brush the vegetable slices with oil once more. Working in manageable batches, arrange the vegetables over the hot barbecue, or on a foil-lined broiler pan. Cook for 3 to 4 minutes, turning them once, or until hot and softened with the edges just beginning to char. Remove from the barbecue or broiler and keep warm while you cook the rest.

Arrange the cooked vegetables on a large warmed platter. Garnish with fresh herbs and lemon wedges. Serve with good crusty bread.

PIZZA OF RADICCHIO, CHÈVRE, TOMATOES, OLIVES, AND CAPERS

I wasn't a great pizza fan until I bought my house in the South of France. In my village there is a small restaurant which specializes in pizzas, salads, and desserts. The pizzas are baked in a wood-fired oven and have the thinnest of crusts. I also learned that pizza toppings don't have to include tomato sauce! Suffice it to say that when I am at home in London I dream of those pizzas. This is my attempt to copy them and, although I only have a normal domestic oven in which to cook them, I am very pleased with the results.

On one occasion, when I couldn't get chèvre (goat cheese), I made this recipe with feta cheese, and it was just as good. Unless you happen to have an enormous oven, the most you will be able to bake is two pizzas at a time, so your guests will have to share as you bake these—or be patient.

6 tbl. EXTRA-VIRGIN OLIVE OIL, PLUS MORE FOR GREASING
1 QUANTITY WHITE HOMEMADE BREAD DOUGH (SEE PAGE 15), LEFT TO RISE
3 SMALL FIRM RADICCHIO HEARTS (USE THE OUTER LEAVES FOR A SALAD)
3 lbs. REALLY RIPE TOMATOES, SLICED
2 MILD ONIONS, THINLY SLICED
12 oz. FRESH GOAT CHEESE (SEE INTRODUCTION), CUT INTO SMALL CUBES (ABOUT 2½ CUPS)
36 PITTED OLIVES (RIPE OR GREEN, OR MIXED)
2 tbl. CAPERS, DRAINED
SALT AND PEPPER

Preheat the oven to 450°. Grease 2 or 3 baking sheets with oil.

Divide the dough into 6 equal portions. Roll these out on a floured surface to make very thin disks about 10 inches across. Arrange these on the baking sheets.

Divide the radicchio, tomatoes, onions, cheese, olives, and capers between the pizza crusts. Drizzle 1 tbl. of olive oil over each.

Season with salt and pepper. Bake for 15 minutes (see introduction), or until the crusts are crisp.

PASSION FRUIT AND PINEAU SYLLABUB WITH BURNED SUGAR SHARDS

A variation on the the great classic British recipe, syllabub. I love this recipe not just because it tastes so wonderful, but because it takes only a few minutes to make.

The sugar shards aren't exactly necessary, but the spectacular result is way out of proportion to the little effort it takes to produce them. Passion fruit are sold in large supermarkets and specialty markets.

⅔ cup *PINEAU DES CHARENTES* (SEE PAGE 97) OR SHERRY
PULP FROM 8 PASSION FRUIT
7 tbl. SUGAR
1¼ cups HEAVY CREAM

Place the *pineau*, 4½ tbl. of the sugar, and the cream in a bowl. Beat until the mixture forms soft peaks. Beat in half the passion fruit pulp.

Pour into 6 wine glasses and chill until required.

Make the sugar shards. Preheat a hot broiler. Cover a baking sheet with foil, making sure it is absolutely smooth. Sprinkle just enough of the remaining granulated sugar over the baking sheet to cover it, but leave a good border uncovered around the edge.

Place the baking sheet under the hot broiler, positioning it as far away from the heat as possible. In 2 to 3 minutes, the sugar will dissolve into a golden liquid caramel. Remove the baking sheet from the broiler and let cool; the caramel will become hard and brittle, like glass. Peel away the foil and break the caramel into "shards."

Just before serving, spoon the remaining passion fruit pulp over the syllabubs. Spear each syllabub with the sugar shards. Serve immediately.

THREE-STAR MEAL

A substantial main course, with accompanying vegetables and sauces, takes center stage in most meals, with the first and last courses playing minor roles. In this elegant menu for a special occasion, however, three mouthwatering sophisticated little dishes vie for attention in successive cameo parts.

ASPARAGUS MOUSSES WITH VEGETABLE BEURRE BLANC

GNOCCHI WITH SPINACH AND PEAS GREEN SALAD

AUSTRALIAN APPLE-CHOCOLATE CAKE

ASPARAGUS MOUSSES WITH VEGETABLE BEURRE BLANC

Although these lovely little molds of creamy asparagus custard are very easy to make, they are absolutely spectacular and taste as wonderful as anything you might be served in the most chic French restaurants.

The sauce will keep warm for up to 30 minutes, if you leave it standing in a pan or bowl of hot water.

2 tbl. BUTTER, PLUS MORE FOR GREASING
1 lb. ASPARAGUS STALKS, BOTTOM
   THIRD TRIMMED OFF
1 SMALL ONION, CHOPPED
3 EGGS
½ cup HEAVY CREAM
SALT AND PEPPER
For the vegetable beurre
   blanc sauce
2 SHALLOTS, FINELY CHOPPED
3 tbl. WHITE WINE
3 tbl. WHITE-WINE VINEGAR
1 cup CHILLED UNSALTED BUTTER,
   CUT INTO 1-inch CUBES
½ cup COOKED FAVA BEANS
⅓ cup COOKED DICED CARROT

Preheat the oven to 375°. Grease 6 small ovenproof molds with butter.

Cook the asparagus in boiling salted water for 8 to 10 minutes, or until tender. Drain, refresh in cold water, and drain again. Reserve 12 tips for the sauce.

Melt the butter in a small heavy-bottomed saucepan over medium heat. Cook the onion, stirring occasionally, until softened.

Whizz the asparagus and onion in a food processor or blender until puréed. With the motor running, gradually add the eggs, followed by the cream. Season with salt and pepper.

Pour the mixture into the prepared molds and cover the top of each with foil. Stand the molds in a bain-marie, or a deep roasting pan half-filled with hot water. Bake for 35 to 40 minutes, or until the mousses are firm.

Meanwhile, make the sauce. Place the shallots, wine, and vinegar in a small saucepan. Simmer them over low heat until reduced to about 2 tbl.; this will take about 5 minutes, but must be done slowly so the shallots cook and give off their flavor.

Over low to medium heat, whisk in the chilled butter, 2 pieces at a time, adding more as soon as they have melted; it should take 3 to 4 minutes to incorporate all the butter. If the sauce begins to bubble, remove the pan from the heat for a moment because the butter will become oily if it is too hot. The finished sauce should be pale, creamy, and emulsified. Season to taste with salt and pepper.

Add the cooked vegetables to the sauce and leave for 1 or 2 minutes to warm them through. Keep warm, if necessary (see introduction).

To serve, unmold the mousses onto 6 warmed plates. Pour the vegetable sauce around them and serve at once.

GNOCCHI WITH SPINACH AND PEAS

These semolina gnocchi are a variation on gnocchi alla romana, *layered with spinach and peas and crusted with bubbling Parmesan. Serve them piping hot, straight from the oven.*

The gnocchi can be made several hours ahead of time and simply put in the oven at the last minute. Buy the semolina from an Italian food store or a health-food store.

18 oz. FRESH SPINACH
7 tbl. BUTTER
4½ cups MILK
1¾ cups SEMOLINA
¾ cup FRESHLY GRATED PARMESAN CHEESE
2 EGGS, LIGHTLY BEATEN
1 cup FROZEN PETITS POIS OR SHELLED PEAS,
   DEFROSTED
SALT AND PEPPER
FRESHLY GRATED NUTMEG

Rinse the spinach and pat it dry.

Melt one-third of the butter over medium heat in a heavy-bottomed saucepan which has a lid. Add the spinach, cover, and cook, shaking the pan occasionally, for about 3 minutes, or until the spinach just wilts. Season it with salt and pepper and a pinch of nutmeg. Drain the spinach in a colander.

Bring the milk and half the remaining butter to a boil in a large saucepan. Add the semolina in a steady stream, stirring constantly to avoid lumps forming. Turn down the heat as low as possible. Season with salt and pepper and a pinch of nutmeg. Simmer for 10 minutes, stirring frequently (this is most easily done with an electric mixer). Stir in half of the Parmesan. Remove the pan from the heat. Let the semolina cool for 1 to 2 minutes. Beat in the eggs.

Using a wet spatula or large knife, and working quickly, spread the semolina on a wet marble or Formica counter to make an even layer about ½ inch thick. Let cool completely; about 1 hour.

Preheat the oven to 425°.

Using a wet 2-inch round cookie cutter or the rim of a small glass, press out circles from the semolina. Place the ''trimmings'' (the little bits between the circles) over the bottom of a greased baking dish.

Spread the cooked spinach over, followed by the peas. Working carefully because the gnocchi circles are fragile, arrange them over the top, slightly overlapping like roof tiles.

Sprinkle with the remaining cheese and dot with the remaining butter. Bake for 15 to 20 minutes, or until golden and bubbling. Serve with a green salad.

AUSTRALIAN APPLE-CHOCOLATE CAKE

Sydney is undoubtedly my favorite city, not just for the weather and the beaches but for all the wonderful restaurants the city boasts. A rising young chef in the restaurant scene there, Dov Soconi, gave me the recipe for this stunning cake, which is light and moist and contains no added fat or flour. It is also incredibly quick and easy. Serve it dusted with confectioners' sugar or with cream and fresh fruit.

4 EGGS, SEPARATED

1 cup PLUS 2 tbl. SUGAR

4 oz. SEMISWEET CHOCOLATE, MELTED

1 DESSERT APPLE, PEELED, CORED, AND GRATED

1 cup VERY FINELY GROUND BLANCHED ALMONDS

VEGETABLE OIL FOR GREASING

Preheat the oven to 350°. Grease a round 8-inch springform cake pan.

Beat the egg yolks with the sugar until light and fluffy. Stir in the sugar, chocolate, apple, and almonds.

Beat the egg whites until stiff. Fold the egg whites into the chocolate mixture.

Pour the batter into the prepared cake pan. Bake for about 45 minutes, or until a toothpick inserted into the cake comes out clean.

Remove the cake from the pan and let cool on a wire rack.

WINTER WARMER

Chase away the chills of winter by indulging in this spicy and comforting menu with more than a hint of influence from Mexico to New England!

REFRIED BEANS WITH MELTED CHEESE AND AVOCADO

CHILI CON FUNGHI AND SPOON BREAD PIE
WILTED WATERCRESS WITH OLIVE OIL AND GARLIC

NEW ENGLAND APPLE SHORTCAKES

REFRIED BEANS WITH MELTED CHEESE AND AVOCADO

Although far from authentic, this recipe is based on a traditional Mexican dish and makes an unusual first course. To serve it as a light lunch or supper dish, add a more substantial salad.

Chili peppers vary enormously in hotness, and how much you should add is very much a matter of personal taste—and endurance! In general, the larger they are, the milder they are; so, in fact, one big one will have roughly the same effect as one small one in the amount of fieriness it adds to a dish.

6 tbl. OLIVE OIL

2 LARGE ONIONS, CHOPPED

2 GARLIC CLOVES, CRUSHED

2 CHILI PEPPERS, SEEDED AND
    FINELY CHOPPED (SEE INTRODUCTION)

5½ cups CANNED RED KIDNEY BEANS,
    DRAINED (ABOUT 1¾ lbs.)

1½ cups GRATED CHEDDAR CHEESE

3 LARGE RIPE AVOCADOS

JUICE OF 2 LIMES

SALT AND PEPPER

To garnish

SALAD LEAVES

LIME WEDGES

SLICED SEEDED CHILI PEPPER
    (OPTIONAL)

Heat two-thirds of the oil in a skillet over low to medium heat. Cook the onions, garlic, and chili peppers, stirring occasionally, for 10 to 15 minutes, or until soft and brown.

Either mash the beans with a fork or whizz them briefly in a food processor or a blender. Add the coarse purée to the contents of the pan. Stir together. Season generously with salt and pepper. Transfer the mixture to a bowl, let cool, and chill.

Form the chilled mixture into 12 burger-shaped patties, about ½ inch thick.

Heat the remaining oil in the skillet. Fry the patties, in manageable batches, for 2 to 3 minutes on each side; keep them warm while cooking the remainder.

Toward the end of this cooking, preheat a hot broiler. Arrange the cooked patties in the broiler pan. Sprinkle with the cheese. Broil until the cheese melts.

Meanwhile, peel, seed, and slice the avocados. Toss the slices lightly in the lime juice.

Arrange 2 patties on each plate, surrounded by the dressed avocado slices. Garnish them with the salad leaves, lime wedges, and chili slices, if using.

CHILI CON FUNGHI AND SPOON BREAD PIE

This recipe is adapted from one I found in an old recipe book. The original "chili" pie filling was "con carne' (made with ground beef), but chopped fresh meaty mushrooms make a perfect substitute, and the finished dish is much lighter and fresher tasting. A few dried mushrooms add a wonderful rich, earthy flavor. Use Chinese dried mushrooms, which are available from Oriental stores, or Italian funghi porcini, which are available from delicatessens and some supermarkets.

Use stoneground cornmeal for the spoon bread, available from delicatessens and some supermarkets. If you can't find any, substitute Italian "easy-cook" polenta, which may be found in Italian food stores and delicatessens.

½ oz. DRIED MUSHROOMS (SEE
    INTRODUCTION)

2 tbl. OLIVE OIL

2 ONIONS, CHOPPED

6½ cups COARSELY CHOPPED MUSHROOMS

1 GREEN BELL PEPPER,
    SEEDED AND COARSELY
    CHOPPED

1 lb. CANNED TOMATOES

4 to 6 FRESH CHILI PEPPERS (DEPENDING ON
    TASTE), SEEDED AND FINELY CHOPPED

2½ cups CANNED RED KIDNEY BEANS,
    DRAINED

CHILI POWDER (OPTIONAL)

SALT AND PEPPER

For the spoon bread topping

2 cups MILK

3 EGGS

2 tbl. UNSALTED BUTTER

⅔ cup CORNMEAL (SEE INTRODUCTION)

½ tsp. SALT

1½ tsp. BAKING POWDER

Soak the dried mushrooms for 30 minutes in 7 tbl. hot water. Drain, reserving the soaking liquid; strain it through cheesecloth or a coffee filter to remove any grit. Chop the mushrooms coarsely.

Heat the olive oil in a saucepan over a medium heat. Fry the onions for 5 to 10 minutes, stirring frequently, until they are soft and translucent. Add the fresh mushrooms and continue to cook, stirring occasionally, for 5 minutes longer, or until the mushrooms begin to soften.

Add the chopped dried mushrooms and their soaking liquid, the pepper, the tomatoes with their liquid, the chili peppers, and the beans. Season with salt and pepper. Cook over medium heat for about 15 minutes, stirring occasionally. The sauce should be quite thick, like spaghetti sauce. If it is too runny, turn up the heat and cook a little longer to evaporate some of the liquid.

Check the seasoning at this stage. If you think you would like a little more "fire," stir in a little chili powder. Pour the sauce into a deep baking dish. Set aside to cool completely.

Preheat the oven to 400°.

Make the spoon bread. Beat ½ cup of the milk with the eggs in a bowl. In a medium saucepan, heat the remaining milk with the butter until it melts. When the mixture comes to a boil, turn down the heat as low as possible and sprinkle in the cornmeal, beating hard to make sure lumps do not form. Add the salt. Remove the pan from the heat and let the mixture cool for 1 to 2 minutes.

Gradually beat the egg mixture into the cornmeal mixture until smooth. Beat in the baking powder.

Pour the batter over the mushroom mixture. Bake for 30 to 40 minutes, until the spoon bread is well risen and golden brown.

WILTED WATERCRESS WITH OLIVE OIL AND GARLIC

Watercress is one of my favorite salad ingredients—I love its strong peppery flavor and attractive dark green leaves. Cooked, it is also an excellent vegetable accompaniment that makes a pleasant change from spinach. There is a traditional French recipe for cooking it with cream, but I prefer this combination with olive oil and garlic.

3 tbl. EXTRA-VIRGIN OLIVE OIL
3 BUNCHES OF WATERCRESS,
    RINSED AND THOROUGHLY
    DRAINED (I USE A SALAD SPINNER)
2 or 3 GARLIC CLOVES (DEPENDING
    ON SIZE), CRUSHED
SQUEEZE OF LEMON JUICE
2 tbl. SLIVERED ALMONDS, TOASTED
SALT AND PEPPER

Heat the oil over medium to high heat in a heavy-based pan which has a lid. Add the watercress, garlic, salt, and pepper. Cover and cook for 1 minute. Stir well, replace the lid, and cook for 2 minutes longer.

Stir again and replace the lid. Remove the pan from the heat and leave the watercress to cook in its own steam for 2 minutes longer.

Pour the contents of the pan into a warmed serving dish. Sprinkle with the lemon juice and toasted almonds.

Serve at once.

NEW ENGLAND APPLE SHORTCAKES

Of course, the most famous and best-loved version of shortcake is strawberry. This more wintry version is filled with spicy apples.

These are good served hot, warm, or cool, but the shortcakes are best as freshly baked as possible.

Makes 8
For the filling
½ tsp. SALT
PIECE OF CINNAMON STICK ABOUT
    4 inches LONG, BROKEN IN
    2 PIECES
2 SLICES OF LEMON
1 to 1¼ cups SUGAR
6 DESSERT APPLES, PEELED, CORED,
    AND SLICED LENGTHWISE
For the shortcakes
4 tbl. BUTTER, PLUS MORE
    FOR GREASING
2½ cups ALL-PURPOSE FLOUR
1 tsp. SALT
2 tsp. BAKING POWDER
1 rounded tbl. SUGAR
⅔ cup MILK
To serve
⅔ cup HEAVY CREAM
1 tbl. SUGAR
¼ tsp. VANILLA EXTRACT

First make the filling. Put the salt, cinnamon, lemon slices, and sugar in a pan with 2½ cups water. Bring to a boil. Add the apple slices. Reduce the heat and simmer for 5 to 10 minutes, or until the apple slices are tender but still hold their shape.

Using a slotted spoon, remove the apples from the pan; reserve. Boil the liquid in the pan until it is reduced to a syrup. Return the apples to the pan; set aside.

Make the shortcakes. Preheat the oven to 450°. Grease a baking sheet with butter.

Sift the flour, salt, baking powder, and sugar into a bowl. Cut in the butter until the mixture resembles fine bread crumbs. Using a fork, mix in the milk and bring the mixture together to form a soft dough. (All this can be done in seconds in a food processor.)

Knead the dough on a lightly floured counter for about 20 seconds, then pat out to a thickness of ½ inch. Using a 3-inch round cookie cutter, cut out 8 circles, rerolling the trimmings as necessary. Place the shortcakes on the prepared baking sheet. Bake for 12 minutes.

Let the shortcakes cool, or serve them hot or warm. If serving hot, reheat the apple filling. Whip the cream with the sugar and vanilla to stiff peaks.

Split the shortcakes across their middle and place a bottom half on each plate. Spoon some apple slices with some syrup over, followed by some of the whipped cream. Replace the tops. Spoon more apples with syrup over and then more cream, piling it as high as possible.

New England Apple Shortcake

FROZEN ASSETS

Every child—whether age eight or eighty—loves ice cream. The iced dessert that ends this rustic menu, however, is a particularly grown-up version, served in a way that will bring a smile of surprise to your guests' faces when they realize that the meal hasn't ended quite as abruptly as they thought!

BOILED GOAT CHEESE ON CORN BREAD WITH MUSHROOM RAGOUT

**AVOCADO AND WALNUT RISOTTO
VERY GREEN SALAD WITH HERB VINAIGRETTE**

CAPPUCCINO ICE CREAM

BROILED GOAT CHEESE ON CORN BREAD WITH MUSHROOM RAGOUT

I have only once entertained a professional chef at dinner—a nerve-racking experience! This was the first course I invented for that occasion. Luckily it was a huge success, and the rest of the evening went like a dream.

The corn bread and the mushroom mixture may be made in advance—the day before if you like—making this a quick-and-easy appetizer for those special occasions when you want to spend as much time as possible with your guests.

Either use fresh, soft individual goat cheeses, which are available from good cheese stores, or slices about ½ inch thick from the kind of chèvre sold in log shapes.

½ oz. DRIED MUSHROOMS (SEE PAGE 108)
2 tbl. OLIVE OIL, PLUS MORE
   FOR GREASING
1 ONION, FINELY CHOPPED
5 cups SLICED MUSHROOMS
2 GARLIC CLOVES, CRUSHED
2 tbl. CHOPPED PARSLEY
2 tbl. HEAVY CREAM
6 SLICES OF CORN BREAD (SEE PAGE
   16), ABOUT ¾ inch THICK
6 SMALL GOAT CHEESES OR SLICES
   OF GOAT CHEESE (SEE INTRODUCTION)
SALT AND PEPPER

Soak the dried mushrooms for 30 minutes in ⅔ cup hot water. Drain, reserving the soaking liquid; strain it through cheesecloth or a coffee filter to remove any grit. Chop the soaked mushrooms.

Heat the olive oil in a saucepan over medium heat. Fry the onion for 5 to 10 minutes, stirring frequently, until soft and translucent.

Add the sliced fresh mushrooms, the garlic, and parsley and continue to cook, stirring occasionally, for 5 minutes longer, or until the mushrooms begin to soften. Add the chopped dried mushrooms and their soaking liquid. Season

with salt and pepper and simmer 2 to 3 minutes longer. Stir in the cream and remove from the heat.

Preheat the oven to 400°. Grease a baking sheet with oil.

Using a round cookie cutter, cut as large a circle as is possible from each slice of corn bread. Arrange these on the prepared baking sheet. Top each with a whole cheese or slice of cheese. Bake for about 5 minutes, or until the cheese is hot and just melting.

Meanwhile, if necessary, reheat the mushroom mixture without letting it boil.

To serve, place a cheese-topped slice of corn bread on each of 6 warmed plates. Spoon the mushroom ragout next to the corn bread. Serve at once.

AVOCADO AND WALNUT RISOTTO

Avocado pears are almost always eaten raw, but they are just as delicious hot. Here their mild flavor and smooth texture contrast with the sharp taste of Parmesan cheese and the crunch of walnuts in a creamy risotto.

These ingredients are far from traditional, but the method of cooking this risotto is quite classic, and will not be completely successful unless you use an Italian risotto rice, such as arborio, which is available from delicatessens and supermarkets.

This risotto should not need extra seasoning because the stock will give it enough flavor and the Parmesan is quite salty.

2 tbl. EXTRA-VIRGIN OLIVE OIL
1 LARGE ONION, CHOPPED
3 GARLIC CLOVES, CRUSHED
1 heaping cup of RISOTTO RICE
   (SEE INTRODUCTION)
ABOUT 2 quarts STOCK
⅔ cup WHITE WINE
¾ cup FRESHLY GRATED PARMESAN CHEESE

2 RIPE AVOCADOS
½ cup CHOPPED WALNUTS
2 tbl. CHOPPED PARSLEY

Heat the oil in a large heavy-bottomed saucepan over medium heat. Cook the onion, stirring, for about 5 minutes, or until it is translucent.

Add the garlic and rice. Stir-fry for 2 to 3 minutes, or until each grain of rice is coated with oil and begins to look translucent.

In another pan, bring the stock to a boil. Leave it over very low heat to simmer.

Pour the wine over the rice and cook over medium heat, stirring constantly, until all the liquid has evaporated.

Ladle enough of the simmering stock over the rice barely to cover it. Cook over medium heat, stirring occasionally, until all the liquid is absorbed.

Continue adding stock this way for 20 to 25 minutes, until all the stock is used and the rice is tender; the risotto should be quite wet and creamy, but with a little "bite" left in the middle of each grain. If all the stock is used before the rice is cooked, add a little boiling water instead.

Just before the rice is fully cooked, stir in half the Parmesan.

At the last minute, peel and dice the avocados, discarding the seed. Fold them gently into the risotto with the walnuts.

To serve, pile the risotto on hot dishes or plates. Sprinkle with the remaining Parmesan and the parsley.

VERY GREEN SALAD WITH HERB VINAIGRETTE

This is an idea or inspiration rather than an exact recipe. Use your imagination, and whatever top-quality green vegetables and salad leaves are available. I might use mixed leaves including lettuce, arugula, and watercress, lightly cooked asparagus, green and fava beans, celery, and avocado.

To 4 tbl. of Vinaigrette (see page 18),

add 1 to 2 tbl. of whatever fresh herbs are available, except sage and rosemary, which are too strongly flavored and not good eaten raw.

Toss the salad mixture in this dressing.

CAPPUCCINO ICE CREAM

I first encountered an ice cream served this way at the Four Seasons restaurant of London's Inn on the Park hotel, where Bruno Loubet—one of the greatest chefs of our time—cooked simply perfect food. This is my version, which is incredibly quick and easy.

If you don't have enough coffee cups that you dare put in the freezer, freeze the ice-cream in small freezerproof glass bowls (or one big one).

Make chocolate shavings by pulling a swivel-bladed vegetable peeler across the top of a block of cold semisweet or bittersweet chocolate.

Makes about 1 ¼ quarts

6 EGG YOLKS (SAVE THE WHITES TO MAKE THE PAVLOVA ON PAGE 53)
4 rounded tsp. INSTANT COFFEE GRANULES
¼ cup SUGAR
1 ¼ cups HEAVY CREAM, WHIPPED UNTIL STIFF
To serve
⅔ WHIPPING CREAM, WHIPPED UNTIL FOAMY BUT NOT STIFF
CHOCOLATE POWDER (UNSWEETENED COCOA POWDER OR DRINKING CHOCOLATE) OR CHOCOLATE FLAKES OR SHAVINGS (SEE INTRODUCTION)

Place the egg yolks in a bowl. Using an electric mixer, beat them for 2 to 3 minutes, or until they are light and fluffy. (You can make this ice cream with a whisk, but it will take twice as long—so find a volunteer to help and take turns as your arms get tired!)

Put ½ cup water, the coffee granules, and sugar in a small pan. Heat until the water is almost boiling and the coffee and sugar dissolve.

Pour this mixture over the beaten egg yolks in a thin steady stream, beating vigorously. Continue to beat until the mixture is cool, increases considerably in volume, and is as thick and foamy as whipped cream; this might take up to 4 to 5 minutes.

Fold in the stiffly whipped cream. Pour the mixture into large freezer proof tea or coffee cups (see introduction). Freeze for at least 8 hours before serving.

Take the ice cream from the freezer 4 to 5 minutes before serving. Place the cups on saucers with spoons. Spoon the whipped cream over. Sprinkle lightly with chocolate powder or chocolate flakes or shavings.

FAST START

In this special-occasion menu, cheese plays an all-important role—appearing at the beginning and the end of the meal. The unusual last course and the fabulous-looking main course both require some time and effort in the kitchen, but the spectacular first course—which will impress the most sophisticated gourmet—takes only moments to prepare and just 3 minutes to cook!

DANIELLE'S BROILED GORGONZOLA IN LEAF PACKAGES

TART OF STUFFED TOMATOES IN PESTO CUSTARD
BEETS, RED ONION, AND PINE NUT SALAD

WARM GOAT CHEESE MOUSSE WITH WALNUTS AND LAVENDER HONEY

DANIELLE'S BROILED GORGONZOLA IN LEAF PACKAGES

As a food writer I am lucky enough occasionally to be taken out for lunch to the latest "in" restaurants by young public-relations women. One such "media glamorpuss" (her words!), who is always in touch with the latest trends in fashionable food, gave me this wonderfully simple recipe. Serve a good tasty bread, like Italian ciabatta, to mop up the juices.

Torta di gorgonzola is an Italian specialty cheese made from layers of fresh gorgonzola cheese sandwiched with creamy mascarpone cheese. It is available from delicatessens and good cheese counters. This recipe is also good made with a creamy goat cheese, and large radicchio leaves work even better than lettuce.

3 SLICES OF *TORTA DI GORGONZOLA*, ½ to 1 inch THICK OR 6 SMALL FRESH GOAT CHEESES OR 6 SLICES FROM A LONG LOG

⅔ cup DRAINED (RESERVING THE OIL) AND COARSELY CHOPPED SUN-DRIED TOMATOES IN OIL

6 LARGE ROMAINE LETTUCE LEAVES

3 tbl. EXTRA-VIRGIN OLIVE OIL

½ cup FRESHLY GRATED PARMESAN CHEESE

½ cup PINE NUTS

BLACK PEPPER

FRESH BASIL LEAVES, TO GARNISH

Chill the slices of cheese for at least 30 minutes. If using *Torta di gorgonzola*, cut each slice in half to make 6 square pieces.

Preheat a hot broiler. Grease the broiler pan with the oil from the sun-dried tomatoes.

Gently pull the wrinkles out of the lettuce leaves and wrap each piece of cheese in one. Place the lettuce and cheese packages on the oiled broiler pan, seam side down.

Brush each one with some of the olive oil and sprinkle with Parmesan and pine nuts. Drizzle with the remaining oil. Add a good twist of black pepper.

Place under the preheated broiler for about 3 minutes, until the Parmesan and nuts are brown but not burned.

Using a pancake turner, transfer the lettuce packages to 6 warmed plates. Surround them with sun-dried tomatoes and garnish with basil leaves. Serve immediately.

LEFT: *Tart of Stuffed Tomatoes in Pesto Custard (page 120)*; RIGHT: *Danielle's Broiled Gorgonzola in Leaf Packages*

TART OF STUFFED TOMATOES IN PESTO CUSTARD

Inspired once more by an Australian recipe, this spectacular-looking tart takes a little time to prepare, but is not difficult and is well worth the effort.

**8 EQUAL-SIZE TOMATOES
    (WEIGHING ABOUT 1 ½ lbs. IN TOTAL)
8 oz. BASIC PIECRUST DOUGH (SEE PAGE 18),
    ROLLED OUT THINLY
1 EGG WHITE, LIGHTLY BEATEN
1 tbl. CORNSTARCH
1 ¼ cups MILK
2 EGGS, LIGHTLY BEATEN
1 tbl. PESTO SAUCE
1 tbl. EXTRA-VIRGIN OLIVE OIL
1 ONION, FINELY CHOPPED
1 cup FINE FRESH BREAD CRUMBS
½ cup GRATED GRUYÈRE CHEESE
1 tbl. CHOPPED FRESH HERBS OF CHOICE
SALT AND PEPPER**

Slice a small "cap" off the stem end of each tomato. Scoop out and discard the seeds and juice and the caps (or add them to a soup or the stockpot).

Dry the insides of the tomato shells with paper towels, then sprinkle lightly with salt. Leave them upturned on several layers of paper towels to drain for 1 hour. Dry the insides again at the end of this time.

Preheat the oven to 375°.

Line a 9-inch loose-bottomed tart pan with the dough. Bake empty for 10 minutes. Brush the tart shell with beaten egg white and return to the oven for 3 minutes longer; this will give a "waterproof" coat to the pastry shell so it remains crisp after the filling is added.

Mix the cornstarch to a paste with a little of the milk. Beat in the rest of the milk, the eggs, and the pesto sauce. Season with salt and pepper.

Heat the oil in a skillet over low to medium heat. Stir-fry the onion for 5 to 10 minutes, until soft and translucent. Remove the pan from the heat and let the onion cool a little. Stir in the bread crumbs, grated cheese, and herbs. Season well with salt and pepper. Use this mixture to stuff the tomatoes.

Pour the custard mixture into the pastry shell. Arrange the tomatoes in the custard, stuffing side up, keeping the tart as neat looking as possible.

Bake for about 30 minutes, or until the custard is set. Serve hot, warm, or at room temperature.

BEETS, RED ONION, AND PINE NUT SALAD

In my view, beets are underrated as a vegetable. Their mild, sweet flavor marries very well with those of other ingredients in mixed salads like this one, which looks as good as it tastes. Pine nuts are available from some supermarkets and delicatessens, but chopped walnuts make a good alternative in this recipe.

**2 cups SLICED COOKED BEETS
2 RED ONIONS, THINLY SLICED
½ cup PINE NUTS
4 tbl. VINAIGRETTE (SEE PAGE 18)
½ tsp. CARAWAY SEEDS
1 tbl. CHOPPED PARSLEY OR SNIPPED CHIVES**

Tart of Stuffed Tomatoes in Pesto Custard

Grease 6 small ramekin dishes or other suitable ovenproof molds with melted butter.

Combine the cheese (including the soft, furry white skin) with the eggs and cream in a blender or food processor. (This can be done by hand but you must first soften the cheese by beating it with a wooden spoon before mixing in the eggs and cream. Then it should be pushed through a strainer to eliminate any lumps.)

Divide the mixture between the molds and smooth the tops. Cover each tightly with a little disk of foil. (The mousses can be prepared in advance up to this stage and kept in the refrigerator for up to 6 hours.)

The mousses can be cooked in 2 ways: either in a bain-marie, or deep roasting pan half-filled with hot water, in an oven preheated to 375° for about 25 minutes; or in a covered steamer over simmering water for about 35 minutes. (I use a Chinese bamboo steamer over a wok.) Either way, they are ready to serve when they are just set.

To serve, turn out the mousses onto warmed plates. Drizzle 1 tbl. of honey over each mousse. Scatter with walnut pieces and serve.

Arrange the sliced beets and onions in a shallow dish. Sprinkle with the pine nuts.

Combine the vinaigrette and caraway seeds. Drizzle the dressing over the beets and onions. Leave for about 1 hour at room temperature to let the flavors develop.

Sprinkle with the chopped herbs just before serving.

WARM GOAT CHEESE MOUSSE WITH WALNUTS AND LAVENDER HONEY

This recipe might sound like a rather odd combination, but I think it's quite stunning. It was inspired by a delicious meal I enjoyed in the Languedoc region of France. To end the meal, we were served pure white rounds of soft fresh goat cheese drizzled with local honey.

1 lb. SOFT GOAT CHEESE

2 EGGS, LIGHTLY BEATEN

4 tbl. HEAVY CREAM

6 tbl. LAVENDER HONEY (OR THE BEST
   FLOWER HONEY YOU CAN FIND)

½ cup CHOPPED WALNUTS

MELTED BUTTER FOR GREASING

THE ITALIAN JOB

The Italian culinary repertoire is perhaps, at least for me, the one that most celebrates the pleasures of eating vegetables. What imagination and variety are shown in the countless recipes producing delicious and satisfying dishes with neither meat nor fish! All who are served this menu will certainly know they have enjoyed an Italian meal, but they probably won't even notice it was a vegetarian one!

"SANDWICHES" OF BAKED EGGPLANT WITH BROILED PEPPERS AND MOZZARELLA

PENNE WITH GOAT CHEESE, SPINACH, FAVA BEANS, AND PEAS ORANGE, OLIVE, AND ONION SALAD

TIRAMISU

"SANDWICHES" OF BAKED EGGPLANT WITH BROILED PEPPERS AND MOZZARELLA

The wonderful combination of flavors in this spectacular, but simple-to-make, appetizer will bring a sunny taste of the Mediterranean to your table. I sometimes make it with soft fresh goat cheeses (one small cheese, split in half, per person).

2 tbl. OLIVE OIL, PLUS MORE
    FOR GREASING
2 LONG, NARROW EGGPLANTS, CUT
    ACROSS INTO 18 THICK SLICES
3 RED BELL PEPPERS
2 TOMATOES, FINELY CHOPPED
4 tbl. VINAIGRETTE (SEE PAGE 18)
12 SLICES MOZZARELLA CHEESE
SALT AND PEPPER
WATERCRESS SPRIGS, TO GARNISH

Preheat the oven to 425°. Grease a baking sheet with some oil.

Place the eggplant slices in a colander. Sprinkle with salt and leave them for 30 minutes to let any bitter juices be drawn out. Rinse thoroughly and pat dry with paper towels.

Brush the eggplant slices on one side with olive oil. Season them with salt and pepper. Arrange the slices in a single layer, greased side up, on the prepared baking sheet.

Bake for 10 to 15 minutes, or until completely soft and golden brown. Remove from the oven and let cool.

Meanwhile, preheat a hot broiler. Cut the peppers into quarters; remove the seeds. Place the pepper quarters, skin side up, in a single layer in the broiler pan. Broil them until all the skins are black. Put them in a plastic bag and let them cook in their own steam for 5 minutes. Remove the charred skin.

Add the chopped tomatoes to the vinaigrette dressing.

Make "sandwiches" using 3 slices of eggplant per portion with a slice of cheese and a slice of pepper between each of the eggplant layers.

Arrange the "sandwiches" on 6 plates. Pour the dressing over. Garnish with watercress sprigs and serve.

PENNE WITH GOAT CHEESE, SPINACH, FAVA BEANS, AND PEAS

20 oz. PENNE (OR OTHER PASTA SHAPE
   OF CHOICE)
¾ cup EXTRA-VIRGIN OLIVE OIL
4 oz. CHUNK OF PARMESAN CHEESE
8 oz. SPINACH LEAVES, TRIMMED
1 cup COOKED PEAS
1 cup COOKED FAVA BEANS
14 oz. GOAT CHEESE, CRUMBLED INTO
   CHERRY-SIZE PIECES
3 tbl. CHOPPED PARSLEY
SALT AND PEPPER

Cook the pasta in boiling salted water according to the directions on the package, until tender but still firm; drain. Sprinkle with 2 tbl. of the oil. Toss well to coat the pasta thoroughly in the oil.

While the pasta is cooking, pare the Parmesan with a swivel-bladed vegetable peeler to make it into shavings.

Heat the remaining oil in a large saucepan or wok. When really hot, add the spinach and stir-fry for 10 seconds. Add the peas and beans and stir-fry for 10 seconds longer.

Add the cooked pasta and the goat cheese. Season well with salt and pepper. Toss together over the heat for another 10 seconds. Serve immediately in warmed plates or dishes, sprinkled with the Parmesan shavings and parsley.

ORANGE, OLIVE, AND ONION SALAD

This great combination of flavors makes a salad which is perfect to serve as a light appetizer, a side salad, or as part of a buffet meal. Any kind of small oranges will do, but use satsumas, a Japanese variety of mandarin oranges, when in season as they are so easy to peel. Any mild onion will do, but use red ones if you see them, because they produce a particularly pretty salad.

6 SATSUMAS (SEE INTRODUCTION),
   PEELED AND THINLY SLICED
2 SMALL ONIONS (SEE INTRODUCTION),
   THINLY SLICED
36 RIPE OLIVES
4 tbl. VINAIGRETTE (SEE PAGE 18)
FEW SALAD LEAVES, TO GARNISH

Put the onion and orange slices and the olives in a bowl. Pour the dressing over. Toss together gently but thoroughly.

Divide between 6 plates. Garnish with salad leaves and serve.

TIRAMISU

Tiramisu seems to be one of the most popular desserts of the moment. There are as many variations as there are restaurants that serve it. This is the best recipe I have tasted and it is also wonderfully easy to make.

4 EGGS, SEPARATED
4 tbl. CONFECTIONERS' SUGAR
3 tbl. BRANDY
2¼ cups MASCARPONE CHEESE
ABOUT 18 LADYFINGERS OR CHAMPAGNE
   COOKIES
ABOUT 1¼ cups VERY STRONG FRESHLY MADE
   COFFEE, COOLED
3 tbl. UNSWEETENED COCOA POWDER

Beat the egg yolks with the sugar until pale and fluffy. Beat in the brandy followed by the cheese.

Beat the egg whites until very stiff. Fold the egg whites into the cheese mixture.

In a deep serving bowl (glass if possible), spread one-third of the cheese mixture in the bottom. Make a layer of cookies, first dipping each one briefly in the coffee (just long enough for them to be soaked, but not too long or they will disintegrate—I find counting "one and," as you dip them in, just the right length of time). Break the cookies in half, if necessary, to fit the corners.

Continue with a layer of another third of the cheese mixture, followed by the other half of the cookies. Finish with the remaining cheese mixture. (There should be 5 layers: 3 of cheese mixture, sandwiching 2 of cookies dipped in coffee.) Smooth the top. Sprinkle with the cocoa.

I like to make this dish in advance and then chill it for a couple of hours before serving it. If doing this, however, it is best to wait until the last moment to sprinkle with cocoa.

INDEX